BLESS OUR SHIP

BLESS OUR SHIP

Mountbatten and
the *Kelly*

RICHARD HOUGH

A John Curtis Book
Hodder & Stoughton
LONDON SYDNEY AUCKLAND TORONTO

British Library Cataloguing in Publication Data
Hough, Richard
Bless our ship : Mountbatten and the "Kelly".
(A John Curtis Book)
1. Great Britain. Royal Navy. World War 2.
Naval operations. Kelly. Ship
2. Mountbatten, Louis Mountbatten, Earl 1900–1979
I. Title
940.545941
ISBN 0-340-54396-5

Published by Hodder and Stoughton,
a division of Hodder and Stoughton Ltd,
Mill Road, Dunton Green, Sevenoaks, Kent TN13 2YA
Editorial Office: 47 Bedford Square, London WC1B 3DP

Designed by Behram Kapadia
Typeset by Hewer Text Composition Services, Edinburgh
Printed in Great Britain by
T J Press (Padstow) Ltd, Padstow, Cornwall

Contents

CONTENTS

Illustrations and Maps

En route from Malta to Crete on 21 May 1941, the *Kelly* launches a depth-charge against a suspected submarine (Imperial War Museum).

The *Kelly* being high-level bombed by the Italians (Imperial War Museum).

Burning Allied supply ships off Crete (Imperial War Museum).

The *Kelly* capsized and sinking (Imperial War Museum).

The *Kipling*'s whaler picking up survivors of the *Kelly* (Imperial War Museum).

Some of the *Kelly*'s survivors in the only carley raft which could be launched before she capsized (Imperial War Museum).

Survivors of the two destroyers cram the decks of the *Kipling* en route to Alexandria (both photos: Imperial War Museum).

Mountbatten goes ashore at Alexandria (Imperial War Museum).

The wounded from the *Kelly* and *Khartoum* being taken off to hospital (Imperial War Museum).

The Price (© Swan Hunter Shipbuilders).

MAPS

For John Curtis, most admirable publisher

The Ancient Bidding*

The Captain:	I call on you to pray for God's blessing on this ship. Bless our ship.
The ship's company:	May God the Father bless her.
The Captain:	Bless our ship.
The ship's company:	May Jesus Christ bless her.
The Captain:	Bless our ship.
The ship's company:	May the Holy Spirit bless her.
The Captain:	What do ye fear, seeing that God the Father, God the Son and God the Holy Spirit is with you?
The ship's company:	We fear nothing.

* A form of service, created in the sixteenth century, to ask God's blessing on a new warship at the time of her commissioning.

Author's Note

I would like to thank the survivors of the *Kelly*'s company and others of the 5th Flotilla ('The Fighting Fifth') who helped me to reconstruct the story of HMS *Kelly* and other destroyers associated with Lord Louis Mountbatten (as he then was) in the 1930s and 1940s. These officers have been especially helpful: Vice-Admiral Sir Peter Ashmore KCB KCVO DSC, Rear-Admiral Philip Burnett CB DSO DSC*, Captain Edward Dunsterville RN (Retd) and Captain Sir Aubrey St Clair-Ford Bt DSO RN (Retd). Lieutenant-Commander J. A. F. Pugsley RN told me about his father, Rear-Admiral A. F. Pugsley CB DSO**, who died while I was writing this book; Captain J. G. 'Jeph' West RN kindly read the manuscript for inaccuracies and infelicities; Kenneth Poolman contributed several quotes from his book *The Kelly* (1954), and Philip Ziegler allowed me to quote several extracts from his official biography of Admiral of the Fleet Earl Mountbatten of Burma (1985).

Preface

I first met Lord Mountbatten, at sea, in January 1971. Over the following years, as I researched and wrote his family history and a dual biography of his remarkable parents, I saw him frequently and listened to him for many hours talking about his life, and especially his active service at sea, of which he was inordinately proud. His period as Captain (D) of HMS *Kelly* and the 5th Flotilla of new destroyers was brief, and the reasons for this are described in this book. His career was to move on to far more exalted levels, but as distinguished old men look back to their boyhood triumphs with special pride and affection, Mountbatten (never the most modest of men) viewed his only period of war service at sea, from September 1939 to May 1941, as if it were the summit of his achievements. His physical fearlessness was legendary, and this was the one time in his life when he was able to demonstrate it at its full flowering.

As a young man, Admiral Beatty had been his greatest hero, and 'doing a Beatty' was his greatest ambition, divulged only to his closest family. They understood what he meant and were as sorry as he was when he was deprived of the opportunity to do so.

I think one of the reasons why he asked me to write about his family was my knowledge of naval history, my specialist subject as a professional writer, which was why I first met him at sea rather than at his home, Broadlands. He was especially proud of his father's naval career and wished to be sure that I understood and appreciated his qualities. During tape-recorded conversations, often in his garden in the fine summer of 1972, it was not long before the subject came round to the Navy, and not long after that to HMS *Kelly*, when a special note of affection came into his voice. Eighteen years later I have been able to make use of these talks, which were so enriching at the time and have so much helped in writing this fiftieth anniversary memorial to the ship and the men who died at her sinking.

PART ONE

THE MAN

1

'This ship is *not* going to sink!'

CAPTAIN LORD LOUIS MOUNTBATTEN

HMS *Kelly* 2305 hrs 9 May 1940
Position 56.48 N. 05.09 E.
(Approx. 100 miles west of north Denmark coast)

Several of the crew of the *Kelly* claimed later that they had seen the dim shape of the German E-boat in the misty darkness, moving slowly. The torpedo it discharged was described by one eye-witness as 'a white line of luminous foam' and by another as 'streaking bubbles'; a third likened the track of the torpedo to a whipping tow-cable rising from the sea.

There were cries of 'Torpedo!' and up on the bridge Captain Lord Louis Mountbatten watched its passage helplessly, dead on target in spite of the high speed at which they were steaming. Many of those on the bridge thought it had been set too deep and was passing under the *Kelly*'s keel. Mountbatten even had time to exclaim, 'Thank God that was a dud!', when there was an almighty explosion right under them. They were all thrown about, and Lieutenant Edward 'Dusty' Dunsterville hit his chin on the voice-pipe hard enough to smash some of his teeth. The torpedo had caught the destroyer on the port side of the forward boiler-room, tearing a rip in the plating some forty feet long.

The explosion was followed instantly by a flash of flame that rose higher than the ship's tripod foremast. A gush of mixed smoke and steam then enveloped the vessel as if to conceal mercifully the horror the explosion had created. The shattered boiler had been developing 20,000 horsepower, and the sea had raged in at twenty-eight knots during the seconds after the impact.

Twenty-seven of the ship's company lay dead, many mutilated or unrecognisably torn to pieces in the ruin of the engine-room; many more were trapped, gravely injured, amongst the torn and twisted steel. Their cries could increasingly be heard as the destroyer finally slowed to a silent halt on the oily swell, the list to starboard so severe that the sea was lapping the starboard gunwale.

At the same moment, the paralysis created by the explosion was broken. Shouted orders rang out in the darkness, and everyone still capable of movement ran to fulfil his role in the damage-control routine. Commander Evans, the Engineer Officer, was first up on the bridge.

'I'm going down to check the damage, sir,' he told his Captain coolly.

'All right, Mike. I'll stay here. I don't think we're going to sink.'

Mountbatten called out through a loudhailer, 'Take over secondary steering,' and listened to the response, 'No answer from the helm, sir.'

The Captain was desperately anxious that some of his men, considering the state of the ship, might abandon her. Repeatedly he called out to reassure them, 'This ship is *not* going to sink!'

Evans was back on the bridge within about three minutes. 'Both boiler-rooms and the after messdeck are full of water,' he reported, 'but the bulkheads on either side seem fairly sound. I'll get them shored up.'

The sound of hammering like machine-guns was heard throughout the ship, and the voices were those of men who might have been under fire. The dim emergency lighting and the silent fans and engines heightened the drama on-board the crippled *Kelly*.

It was an act of survival not surrender when the torpedo crews fired off all ten of the twenty-one-inch torpedoes and discharged at 'safe' every depth-charge. The ready ammunition for the 4.7-inch guns was hurled into the sea, too, stripping the destroyer of her fire-power. All the boats were lowered and cast off, all but the whaler which was set to tow.

Below decks the rescue of trapped men was the first activity. There was nothing to be done for the engine-room staff; they were all dead in the oily, bloody shambles. But there was hope for some in the wireless office, which had been shattered and the entrance blocked off, except for a narrow crack through which a rescue party and the doctor could hear groans and cries.

Attempts were made to open the gap with a broken stanchion. It was still not wide enough for the doctor to get through, but a telegraphist named O'Neill, who was no more than a boy, said, 'I'm only skinny – shove me through.' The doctor handed him a hypodermic syringe full of morphia. After O'Neill had squeezed through the twisted metal plate, it was seen to close under some mighty unknown pressure and the telegraphist was as trapped as the others inside.

Down on the tiller flat another party was struggling with the emergency steering, pumping the rudder hard to port and then starboard to no useful effect. The sick-bay had been split open, the ward-room was flooded, and the doctor was giving morphia and dressing wounds far aft. Most of the victims were burnt and some were not going to live. When Mountbatten found a terribly burnt seaman lying unobserved on deck, he took off his greatcoat and laid it over him.

Mountbatten had seen another destroyer bearing down on his crippled ship, which had all her fighting lights on. The high-pitched noise of her fans sharpened the threat of imminent disaster, but it was no enemy. HMS *Bulldog* had been working with the *Kelly* before the attack and now Mountbatten ordered her to take the *Kelly* in tow.

A while later, one of *Kelly*'s sister ships, the *Kandahar*, came close alongside, too. By chance, the officer of the watch was

Mountbatten's nephew, twenty-one-year-old David, Marquis of Milford Haven, who had seen the effects of the torpedo hit and assumed that the *Kelly* had gone down beneath the flames and clouds of smoke. Mountbatten signalled her to come back at daylight and take off the wounded.

There was quite a swell getting up, adding to the trials of the *Kelly*'s men and to the difficulties of getting a line aboard from the *Bulldog*. But soon after midnight the towing-cable was secured, and slowly the waterlogged, wrecked and helpless destroyer was eased into motion. The wounded felt nothing of this silent passage, which built up to six knots, but were encouraged when told that they were on their way home.

A few minutes after midnight on 10 May a strange event occurred, adding a bizarre and mysterious touch to the night's events. A German E-boat raced out of the darkness towards the labouring *Bulldog*. She struck her a glancing blow and sped on at some forty knots towards the *Kelly*, hitting her well forward on her crippled side and tearing at everything in her path – davits, guardrails and other equipment – while leaving behind large sections of her hull, belts of 20 mm. ammunition and her wheel. Several men who saw the wreck fly off into the darkness like a Valkyrie swore that they heard the screams of the men as they plunged to their death. If it was the E-boat which had torpedoed them an hour earlier, then retribution had come fully and swiftly to the crew.

While on not-far-distant land the German Panzers advanced and broke through the Dutch, Belgian and French defences, signalling the invasion that was to give the Germans their greatest victory, by 5 a.m. the *Kelly* and *Bulldog* struggled on. Already the tow had twice parted and been reinstated, and it would be some ninety hours more before they could reach safety. Meanwhile, as day follows night, Mountbatten knew that the German bombers would arrive overhead, like crows for their carrion.

2

'The strength of twice three thousand horse'

RUDYARD KIPLING

D ickie Mountbatten's career was never in doubt, even from his earliest days. 'It never at any remote moment ever entered my mind,' he once told this writer, 'it never even occurred to me – I had no other plans whatsoever than go into the Navy.' Many officers before the 1914–18 war came from naval families that went back many generations, and the same names could be found in the naval lists of 1912 as in 1770, like Arbuthnot and Troubridge. This was not the case with young Mountbatten. His father had been born in Hesse, a German land-locked state not notable for its maritime tradition. But Prince Louis of Battenberg as a child had developed an inordinate enthusiasm for the British Royal Navy.

The Hessian connections with Queen Victoria and her family ensured that this eccentric wish of Prince Louis's was met, and at the age of fourteen he travelled to England, was granted British citizenship and joined the Royal Navy. Being of such elevated rank was as much a disadvantage as an advantage, and this young officer had many prejudices to overcome, not least his German accent, of which he was never able to rid himself.

But Prince Louis had a good brain and immense charm, and prospered socially and in the service. After a flaming affair with Lillie Langtry, which produced a child, he married Princess Victoria, the daughter of the Queen's daughter, Alice, and of the Grand Duke of Hesse. She was as bright as a button, and the two boys from the marriage were exceptionally well endowed with looks and brains. George, Dickie's elder brother by eight years, considered no other career than the Royal Navy, just like his father and younger brother. When Dickie first went to Osborne Naval College as a cadet in May 1913, 'Georgie' was a lieutenant in the battle-cruiser *New Zealand*. Dickie worshipped him and his love and admiration for his father, now at the very top of the Navy as First Sea Lord, were immense.

The British Navy of 1913 was by far the most powerful in the world, and had been since Napoleonic days and earlier, its nearest rival being the German Navy, which had recently made serious efforts to challenge this superior strength. But the Royal Navy had the singular disadvantage of having lived on its history and tradition for too long without a serious war. It had also resisted every new material and technological advance since it was first threatened with steam-power in place of wind-power. The Navy's senior admirals had all been brought up under sail and most of them detested torpedoes, mines and especially submarines, which a senior admiral once described as 'underhand, unfair and damned un-English'. Winston Churchill, who had gone to the Admiralty as First (political) Lord at the end of 1911, complained of 'a frightful dearth of first-class men in the Vice-Admirals' and Rear-Admirals' lists'.

One exception was David Beatty, Churchill's Naval Secretary, who wrote disparagingly that 'we have eight Admirals, and there is not one among them, unless it is Prince Louis, who impresses me that he is capable of a great effort'. But the further down the ranks you looked, the brighter the picture, and there were numbers of intelligent, enterprising, resourceful and courageous men among the captains and commanders.

At the age of thirteen, Cadet His Serene Highness Prince Louis of Battenberg (as Dickie, like his father before him, was formally listed) was already determined to emulate his father and one day become First Sea Lord. But, as his mother reminded him, he would have to pull himself together if he was going to get anywhere worthwhile. He tended to be lazy and slapdash in his work, and come out in exams somewhere near the bottom, both at his preparatory school and now at Osborne.

Dickie's arrival at Osborne, his title and name embossed upon his trunk, created a minor sensation, because he was both a cousin of the King and the son of the First Sea Lord. He was also rather small for his age, and there was a vulnerability about his pretty face. His parents warned that he might be bullied, and so he was. But he was perfectly capable of looking after himself, and the bullying suddenly ceased when he fought an older boy and tormentor, and beat him soundly. 'I've become a hero,' he told his mother, in an early expression of immodesty.

Life at Osborne was tough enough without the bullying; discipline was as severe as the corporal punishment for not adhering to it. A lashing was nothing like as bad as in Nelson's time when a cat-o'-nine-tails was used, but it was quite bad enough for this tender age. Dickie stood up to it well.

By contrast, at the end of his first term, and showing off his cutaway jacket for the first time, this thirteen year old was warmly welcomed into the arms of his family at Schloss Heiligenberg on the Rhine for the summer holiday. Fellow guests were the Emperor of Russia and his wife, Dickie's aunt, the Empress ('that crazy lunatic', as he later called her), their daughters, and a great number of uncles and aunts and their children, every one to be found with their amazingly complicated titles in the *Almanac de Gotha*.

'Oh, they were lovely and terribly sweet,' Mountbatten described the Czar's daughters, 'far more beautiful than their photographs show. I was crackers about Marie, and was determined to marry her. She was lovely.' As an old man, he pointed to her photograph in his bedroom: 'I have always kept her there.'

Other photographs evoking that summer of 1913 were of another aunt, Irène, who had married Prince Henry of

Prussia, a German grand-admiral and the Emperor of Germany's brother; Tsar Nicholas II, King George V's look-alike; and many more who, in less than a year, were to be embroiled in the greatest war in history on different sides. 'They were all charming, every one of them,' Mountbatten recalled in 1972.

Everything that the hierarchy of Germany, Britain and Russia did during that last summer of peace had a symbolic and prophetic element. After games and riding, evening dancing and happy family chat in Hesse, they all moved up to Kiel, the German naval base, and embarked on the Russian *Standart*. 'It was a beautiful yacht,' Mountbatten remembered, 'with every conceivable comfort. We all went on-board and were given the most lavish cabins – very different from Osborne where we slept forty to a wooden hut.'

Then for Dickie it was back to the austerities and hard labour of Osborne until Christmas, when there was a brief break again amidst the comforts and love of family life. Three days after Dickie's fourteenth birthday – 25 June – the cadets learned of the assassination of the Austrian Archduke Franz Ferdinand and his wife at Sarajevo, which was apparently a serious business though they did not all understand why.

This far-away tragedy added an ominous note to the Royal Navy Review at Portsmouth shortly afterwards. Third only to the King himself and Churchill as civil First Lord of the Admiralty, Prince Louis as First Sea Lord was the most important officer present; and at his side, looking absurdly young, stood Dickie.

'It took more than six hours', Churchill wrote of this historic event, 'for this armada, every ship decked with flags and crowded with bluejackets and marines, to pass with bands playing and at fifteen knots before the Royal Yacht, while overhead the naval seaplanes circled continuously.'

'Men o'war were to be a part of the fabric of my life for the next half century,' said Mountbatten, 'but I would never again see a sight like this. No one had beaten us at sea for centuries, and how could they now, against all this might? That's what was going through my mind.'

There was a sham fight after the inspection, and Dickie was invited by his brother into his twelve-inch gun turret. 'It was great fun,' recalled the cadet, describing how he was allowed to train and elevate the guns. Characteristically, he claimed two victories without firing a shot: 'I am sure I did for the *Lord Nelson* and *Drake.*'

The big ships, the 25,000-ton battleships and battle-cruisers, fascinated him, but it was the flotillas of destroyers that held his attention most closely. There were almost a hundred of them present, lean and painted black, with three stubby funnels, four-inch gun on the forecastle, and torpedo-tubes amidships ready to swing to port or starboard. He knew that they could turn on a penny, going from full ahead to full astern in thirty seconds.

'I knew I still had another term ahead of me at Osborne, then a year or more at Dartmouth,' Mountbatten recounted, 'but how I longed to put up my midshipman's patches for the first time and serve in the fleet in one of the flotillas!'

He would have agreed with a fellow officer, Rear-Admiral D. Arnold-Forster, when he wrote later:

> It is in the small craft, the destroyers, sloops and gunboats, that the spirit of adventure in the Navy thrives best, for small ships penetrate where big ships cannot. And in the destroyer service especially there is an element of glamour and daring that appeals to those with strong sea instincts.

This same officer added some other observations on life in a destroyer, in which accommodation below was so restricted by the huge turbine engines, and conditions on deck in heavy weather more like those of a submerging submarine:

> When one of these little destroyers was in company with a big ship, the speed ordered was a matter for the discretion of the captain of the latter. A destroyer captain would seldom take the initiative in asking permission to ease down on account of the weather. Still, some mornings it annoyed him when clinging to the twelve-pounder on

his little bridge, with the boat shaking her stern in the air, taking seas over the narrow forecastle, and throwing solid chunks of spray over the bridge and down the funnels, to see nicely-dressed officers appear after a good breakfast on a bone-dry quarter-deck, and amuse themselves by watching his antics through glasses – the chaplain probably taking photographs to send home! When things on deck were being smashed up, crockery and breakfast gone to blazes, galley fire out – it was a relief when the big ship thought of reducing speed.

The origins of the destroyer, which reached its pre-Second World War apotheosis in the *Kelly*, lay in the age-old search for a more decisive means of sinking a ship than by cannon-ball or shell. The fireship was an early attempt, but the result was usually more psychological than material, though it was significantly successful against the Spanish Armada at Calais in 1488. Three hundred years later in the American War of Independence a Captain David Bushnell of Connecticut designed a boat 'for the purpose of conveying magazines to the bottom of hostile ships and there exploding them'. It did not work.

Samuel Colt, Robert Fulton, two Royal Navy officers, both called Harvey, and others took their lives in their hands with experimental mines and harpoon torpedoes, manually guided explosive charges at the end of a long pole, somewhat pretentiously named 'the Spar Torpedo'. A naval manual of the time did not compromise in its description: 'The guiding principle of the Spar Torpedo', ran the instructions, 'is that its construction and design render it necessary that wherever the torpedo goes the operator must go too.'

An expatriate Englishman and an Austrian inventor, working separately, were not satisfied that this was the right way to go. Robert Whitehead was an engineer and designer at his own works in Milan. He invented pumps to drain the Lombardy marshes and numerous other ingenious machines, but learned to his disgust that all his patents were annulled by the revolutionary Government of 1848.

Whitehead packed away his tools and drawings and headed

for Austria. This enterprising man soon busied himself with marine engines for the Austrian Navy, and at the Battle of Lissa the Austrian flagship and other men o'war were powered by Whitehead engines. As a result, he was much honoured by the Austrian Government.

Among his admirers was a Captain Lupuis of the Austrian Navy, who had conceived the idea of an automobile torpedo which would dispense with the need for a semi-suicidal operator and replace him with an engine and guidance system. He consulted Whitehead about this, but the Englishman told him that it would not work. However, after Lupuis had left, Whitehead seems to have changed his mind. For the following two years, he worked with only his son and one mechanic secretly developing the first automobile torpedo. That was in 1867: fifty years later in the Great War, torpedoes derived from this prototype were sinking British merchantmen at a monthly rate of some 700,000 tons, bringing his country to the edge of starvation.

By the time the British Admiralty had heard about Whitehead's invention – his submersibles as he called them – the charge of gun cotton in the nose had been increased to sixty-seven pounds, the range to 1,000 yards and the running depth could already be varied from five to fifteen feet. It was powered by a compressed-air engine, and was fourteen feet long and sixteen inches in diameter. Asked in 1870 to demonstrate his weapon on the River Medway, Whitehead had no trouble in sinking a hulk at first try. The British Government bought the manufacturing rights on the spot for £15,000. Soon half the world's navies were building Whiteheads, and the torpedo grew bigger and more destructive year by year.

Whitehead originally envisaged his torpedo as a weapon to be lowered into the water from a small boat by dropping-gear, and it was some time before the torpedo-tube allowed a launch to be made while the boat was in motion. The faster the boat's speed, the more effective the weapon: this was recognised by a number of launch builders in Britain, notably Alfred Yarrow, John I. Thornycroft and J. S. White. Thornycroft was first in the field with the *Lightning*, the first ever commissioned torpedo-boat. This midget man o'war, eighty-four feet long, with a speed of nineteen knots and carrying a torpedo-tube on deck at the bow and dropping-gear amidships, was the progenitor of the hundreds of lethal torpedo-carrying boats which changed the nature of war at sea in a few decades, at first threatening and then making obsolete the steel battleship.

The British monopoly lasted months rather than years. By 1892 these were the numbers of torpedo-boats built by the leading naval powers:

France	220
Britain	186
Russia	152
Germany	143
Italy	129

It was now horribly clear that quite a small navy could buy or build torpedo-boats for under £25,000 which could cripple a major navy with battleships costing close to a million pounds. The counter-defence came in various forms: heavier underwater protection, steel netting suspended from booms round a battleship at anchor or moored ('crinolines'), and the fitting of multiple, light quick-firers, just as fifty years later American battleships in the Pacific were protected from Japanese aeroplanes by as many as two hundred anti-aircraft guns.

Finally, there was the destroyer, a much bigger ship intended to double-up the functions of a torpedo-boat and a torpedo-boat destroyer. HMS *Daring* of 1893 displaced 260 tons and was armed with a single, quick-firing twelve-pounder and three six-pounders. She had a submerged bow torpedo-tube and two dropping-gear amidships. With a speed of over twenty-seven knots, she could overtake any contemporary torpedo-boat.

The *Daring* and six more of her class, followed at once by twenty-seven more, caught the public imagination as darting giant-killers. They featured in stories in the *Boys' Own Paper* and in the illustrated magazines, swept by spray of their own making, black funnel smoke streaming astern.

In 1897, Rudyard Kipling wrote 'Destroyers', the opening verse of which ran:

> The strength of twice three thousand horse
>   That seeks the single goal;
> The line that holds the rending course,
>   The hate that swings the whole:
> The stripped hulls, slinking through the gloom,
>   At gaze and gone again –
> The Brides of Death that wait the groom –
>   The Choosers of the Slain!

At the turn of the century a fleet action was still envisaged as a gunnery duel between two parallel opposing lines, as practised for centuries, but now with a new element of darting attacks by torpedo-boats opposed by equally swift counter-attacks by destroyers. It was also accepted that the torpedo-craft would damage or sink many battleships. At least the submarine was not yet a threat, though far-sighted admirals could already discern more trouble in the future; and the aeroplane was but a twinkle in the Wright brothers' eyes.

The first naval power to demonstrate the worth of torpedo-craft in warfare was Japan in 1895 in her war with China. After the Japanese gained a considerable advantage at sea at the Battle of the Yalu in 1894, on two successive nights at the Chinese base at Weihaiwei, Japanese torpedo-craft succeeded in attacking four Chinese warships, disabling them and thus gaining total control of the sea.

If the Chinese could hardly be classed as a worthy opponent for the growing and zealous Japanese Navy, the Russian Navy of 1904 certainly was, at least in total strength. Like Admiral Yamamoto in 1941, Admiral Heihachiro Togo had long since prepared secret plans for a surprise assault on the enemy fleet as a prelude to war against Russia. This was to be a night torpedo-boat attack on the Russian fleet in Port Arthur, which was carried out on 8 February 1904. A powerful force of well-trained men in destroyer and torpedo flotillas entered the harbour without any difficulty and with full knowledge of the position of every Russian warship.

They were guided by the lights on shore and on the Russian ships, which were lit from stem to stern as if for some regatta. Before a gun opened fire, the fourteen-inch Whiteheads were hissing across the harbour waters from the Japanese boats, crippling two of Russia's best battleships and a cruiser. Like Pearl Harbor thirty-seven years later, it was all over within a few minutes, and the cost to the attackers was negligible.

Great and decisive gunnery actions at the Battle of Japan Sea (14 August 1904) and Tsu-Shima (27–28 May 1905) were fought with little intervention from the torpedo. But it was the torpedo that changed the balance of power at sea in this war – the greatest war at sea since the Trafalgar campaign 100 years earlier.

In all the navies of the world the lessons of the Russo–Japanese War were taken to heart, above all the success of the torpedo-boat and destroyer, and also of mines, which had claimed many victims. Both Britain and Germany, in 1905 building up to the climax of their competition at sea, laid down numerous destroyers to accompany the fleet for attack and defensive purposes.

Take the first British 'Tribal' class as an example, designed in the closing stages of the war in the Far East. Size had increased to around one thousand tons, and the speed to thirty-four or thirty-five knots, quite as fast as any British destroyer built thirty years later for the Second World War. This increase was brought about by the introduction of oil-fired boilers and turbines, and one of the conditions laid down by the Director of Naval Construction was that these 'Tribals', thirteen in all, must be able to steam at thirty-three knots for eight hours in a moderate sea, an inconceivable requirement ten years earlier.

The last destroyers launched before the outbreak of the First World War were not as fast as the old 'Tribals', but their offensive power, in guns and torpedoes, had greatly increased. The Germans had long since introduced a 4.1-inch gun with a high muzzle velocity and a range of close to twelve thousand yards, or nearly seven miles. As this made the British twelve-pounder, or three-inch, obsolete as far as destroyer action was concerned, the four-inch gun had been introduced. In 1910, the bore of the torpedo had also been increased to twenty-one inches. It was twenty-two feet long and carried a charge of 280 pounds. Its range was 10,000 yards at thirty knots and 5,000 yards at forty knots.

The most numerous destroyers at the great Fleet Review shortly before the opening of the First World War were of around 750 tons with two four-inch and two twelve-pounder guns, and two twenty-one-inch torpedo-tubes, whose speed was a little over thirty knots. These were the boats upon which Mountbatten had feasted his eyes when, as a fourteen-year-old cadet, he accompanied his father to the Royal Review.

3

'If you'll put the helm over now, sir, you'll get the next one all right'

HMS *BROKE'S* NAVIGATOR

I f Mountbatten's heart's desire had been met and he had served in destroyers in the 1914–18 war, there were many roles which his ship might have been ordered to play. The most likely was with the Grand Fleet and Battle-Cruiser Squadron (later BC Fleet). According to the Grand Fleet Battle Orders, their business was to defend the big ships from some sixty enemy destroyers, which the Germans called torpedo-boats because their relative torpedo strength to guns was higher than that of Admiral Jellicoe's eighty destroyers in six flotillas.

But in the heat of the Battle of Jutland these orders were disregarded and both Jellicoe and the C-in-C Battle-Cruisers, Admiral Sir David Beatty, launched attacks against the German line. These attacks could only be compared with a cavalry charge and were equally invigorating and dangerous. The first occurred during the battle-cruiser action at a time when Beatty had had two of his big ships blown up and was anxious to force the German ships to turn away to give time for his fifteen-inch-gunned 5th Battle-Cruiser Squadron to close the range.

The British destroyers were led by Commander the Hon. E. B. S. Bingham in the *Nestor*, thirteen of them in all. The Germans replied with an equally determined counter-attack with fifteen boats. Almost immediately the little dark destroyers, all at full speed, were engaged in a gunnery duel down to a range of less than half a mile while they attempted to launch their torpedoes. The official account ran:

It was a wild scene of groups of long low forms vomiting heavy trails of smoke and dashing hither and thither at thirty knots or more through the smother and splashes, and all in a rain of shell from the secondary armament of the German battle-cruisers, as well as from the [light-cruiser] *Regensburg* and the destroyers, with the heavy shell of the contending squadrons screaming overhead. Gradually a pall of gun and funnel smoke almost hid the shell-tormented sea, and beyond the fact that the German torpedo attack was crushed, little could be told of what was happening.

Both sides lost two of their destroyers, but the British charge had the intended effect of forcing the enemy battle-cruisers out of line besides hitting the German battle-cruiser *Seydlitz* with a single torpedo. It did not knock the big ship out of the battle, but it caused some damage and, according to the German history, 'forced the German battle-cruisers to turn away at the decisive moment'.

There were other mass attacks by destroyers on both sides, and the losses were heavy. Like the Germans, the British fleet during daylight hours suffered only a single, non-fatal hit from a torpedo, but the fear of the destroyers' torpedoes on both sides governed the movements of the big ships and was largely instrumental in depriving Admiral Jellicoe of a famous victory.

The British commanders always complained of a lack of destroyers and this was because they had so many functions to fill. That other torpedo-carrying boat, the submarine, was in part responsible for this. So terrible had losses of merchantmen to U-boats become that convoys, employed so successfully in the Napoleonic wars, had reluctantly to be reintroduced, and although other craft were rushed into production, the main burden of escorting convoys rested on the destroyer. With her high speed she could race to a suspected area where a U-boat might be lurking to attack. At first her only weapons were gunfire and her ability to ram when the enemy was on the surface, but with the urgent invention and introduction of the depth-charge, exploding underwater at pre-set depths, chances of making a 'kill' were much increased.

Convoys cut down the rate of losses, but the demand for destroyers and other escort vessels stretched British ship-building facilities to the utmost. As many as 299 destroyers were launched between the first day of war and the armistice on 11 November 1918.

Besides those two vital functions, destroyers were employed on coastal patrol work – 'Patrol Flotillas' and 'Local Defence Flotillas' – operating from such bases as Harwich, Dover, Portsmouth, Chatham, the Humber, the Tyne, the Forth and Devonport. By far the most active of these were the flotillas at Harwich and Dover. The Harwich force, with the 5th Light-Cruiser Squadron, was commanded throughout the war by the fiery and enterprising Commodore Sir Reginald Tyrwhitt. It was responsible for the southern part of the North Sea and conducted reconnaissance as far as the Bight of Heligoland, escorting the weekly Dutch neutral convoy, intercepting German light forces and coastal convoys, and while at sea at all times looking out for U-boats. Although, to his fury, Tyrwhitt missed the Battle of Jutland, his was one of the liveliest of commands and acquired a reputation for derring-do with the British public.

Tyrwhitt often operated jointly with his next-door neighbour at Dover, the colourful and determined Captain E. R. G. R. Evans with his 'Dover Patrol'. The 6th Patrol Flotilla was responsible for guarding the entrance to the English Channel, escorting the never-ending traffic of troop transports, hospital ships and supply ships across the Channel, patrolling the Belgian coast and escorting the monitors which frequently bombarded it, hunting U-boats, and laying and safeguarding net barrages against them. Like the Harwich flotilla, it always had some function to perform.

Evans was always inadequately equipped to deal with all these operations.

The Patrol Flotilla attached to Dover Straits [he wrote] consisted of twelve very fast destroyers classed as the 'Tribals', and in addition to these we had a dozen or so of small, obsolete, torpedo-boat destroyers.

Although navally known as 'thirty-knotters', these little vessels were virtually incapable of exceeding twenty-five knots at full speed. Some of them were built as far back as 1896, and in 1914 they were in various stages of decay. . . . Their captains and officers were proud of them nevertheless; their crews were happy and their sub-lieutenants, boys of twenty, spent hours in hiding the dented and patched disfigurements of age by a liberal use of black paint. . . . The big-handed sailor men were proud of their floating homes, and they willingly put up with the most dreadful accommodation in the dark, ill-ventilated hole, officially named the mess-deck, for the greater freedom from big-ship discipline, and the considerable increase to their scanty pay.

Evans's exploits in the Channel were in the spirit of 'Taffrail' and G. A. Henty, and earned him the sobriquet 'Evans of the *Broke*', the *Broke* being his big flotilla leader which took part in so many close actions with the always more numerous German boats. His most famous action was on the night of 20 April 1917, when in company with the *Swift* they met six German destroyers of the most modern type. There was a brisk gunnery duel and Evans then conned his ship to ram one of the Germans while continuing to fire with his fore four-inch guns. Meanwhile, his Torpedo Officer had launched a torpedo at point-blank range and a few seconds later exclaimed triumphantly above the din, 'We've got her!'

There was a massive explosion, and 'I put my helm hard aport and swung away to starboard for a matter of seconds. . . .' Suddenly his Navigator called out, 'If you'll put the helm over now, sir, you'll get the next one all right.'

And this was what happened. 'Our strong bow ground its way into the enemy vessel's flank; in the blaze of gun flashes we read her name, *G42*, as her bow swung round towards us, while we carried her bodily away on our ram,' Evans described. The German crew attempted to board the *Broke*, more to escape the holocaust than to try to capture the British ship.

'Repel boarders!' the officers cried out, the first time such an order had been heard for a hundred years. Always prepared for this eventuality, Evans had ordered rifles with fixed bayonets, revolvers and cutlasses to be ready for use, and all were much employed in the next few minutes.

The *Broke* eventually had to be towed back to Dover, much damaged and with many casualties. The report of this fight, with all its close-action heroism and shades of Nelson at St Vincent, scarcely affected the course of the war but greatly heartened the nation at a time of deep gloom and depression. War weariness had set in, and U-boats sank a record total of one million tons of shipping during this month of April 1917.

To set against this on the credit side was the entry of the United States into the European war. The Americans possessed the third most powerful navy in the world and had a great number of destroyers and small patrol vessels, which would be of invaluable support. The Prime Minister, David Lloyd George, was at this time engaged in an internal battle with Admiral Jellicoe, now First Sea Lord, who was showing every reluctance to introduce the convoy system. One of the Admiral's arguments was that convoys would demand too many patrol vessels and destroyers that could not be spared from the Grand Fleet. But by mid-July 1917 the first eighteen US destroyers had arrived from across the Atlantic, and many more were on their way. These were mostly 'Flivvers', 'Flussers' and 'Thousand Tonners', not outstanding vessels but fully adequate for escort work and for working with the American Battle Squadron of five dreadnoughts under the command of Rear-Admiral Hugh Rodman.

Instead of service in one of those tempting destroyers at Spithead, it was back to school for Dickie Battenberg. On 4 August 1914, the night war broke out with Germany, the First Sea Lord and his younger son had dined alone at the Admiralty. Out in the streets the crowds cheered and moved like a river in full flood down the Mall to Buckingham Palace.

'I felt half excited and elated, half sorry for my father and very sorry that I was only fourteen,' Mountbatten recalled. Back among his fellow cadets more elation and blind optimism prevailed. Soon, surely, there would be an enormous battle in the North Sea, and like Nelson at Trafalgar, there would be a smashing victory and it would all be over by Christmas.

It did not turn out like that at all. The first reality of war was the loss of three big cruisers to one German submarine. Among the 1,200 drowned were many senior cadets who were known to them and their teachers. In another sinking, the Osborne doctor who was much loved and respected was killed. 'That night I cried myself to sleep,' Dickie wrote to his mother. In the Mediterranean, a German squadron escaped from more powerful British and French forces, and the threat of enemy submarines forced the entire British Grand Fleet to abandon its main base at Scapa Flow.

What was the supposedly omnipotent and all-powerful Royal Navy up to, the public was beginning to ask. It sought a scapegoat and found one in the First Sea Lord himself, German-born and a frequent visitor in the past to that now enemy country, where he had all his property and where his wife's brother-in-law was a grand-admiral in the German Fleet.

There were mutterings in London's clubland, especially among retired admirals who had been passed over for appointments gained by Prince Louis, not least the highest command of them all. Hints appeared in the press about the 'Germhun' in our midst. The tide of suspicion inevitably reached Osborne, where accusations were less restrained. 'I got rather a rotten time of it for about three days as little fools insisted on calling me a German spy,' Dickie wrote home.

As an old man, Mountbatten loved to relate how he reacted to the news that his father had resigned – or had, in effect, been dismissed by Churchill. 'I marched out alone on the parade-ground at Osborne and stood at attention at the base of the flagpole, the tears coursing down my cheeks.' At that moment of grief and humiliation, he had determined to right a great wrong.

The scene has all the features he most cherished and wished others to relate to him: loyalty to family, service and nation; unashamed sentiment and ambition. It is almost too good to believe, and yet he always insisted on its truth, and it has been recorded in every biography of him, written and on film. Asked by this writer whether the occasion was a turning-point in his life, steeling him to emulate his father, he replied typically and circuitously, 'Too many people say they have heard me say in the past, "I am going to right a great wrong" or something like that, for it not to be true.'

At Osborne Naval College, and later at Dartmouth, Dickie Battenberg was noted more for the number of his accidents than for his record. At Osborne he passed out thirty-fifth of eighty, but he did better from Dartmouth – eighteenth of eighty – even though he had had to take his exams lying in plaster with a broken leg. Earlier, he had broken his ankle trying to learn skating in half the time of anyone else. When at length he put up his midshipman's patches for the first time, he was appointed not to a destroyer but to Admiral Beatty's HMS *Lion*, just repaired from her damage at the Battle of Jutland.

His chagrin at missing this battle was more intense than his disappointment at not getting a destroyer. After all, Beatty was his hero, and to serve under him was a great honour. Moreover, he did see some action in the North Sea before he pleaded with his father to use his influence. It was not just the higher pay and longer leaves that were the privileges of destroyer service. There was more rapid promotion and a greater chance of meeting the enemy – and earning medals for heroism. His father agreed, as he believed strongly that a young midshipman could do no better than serve in the flotillas for a while at least.

In 1917, the name Battenberg was changed to the less German-sounding Mountbatten, just as the Royal Family

woke up one morning as the Windsors to cleanse any asso-
ciations with the enemy. Thus it was that Dickie, as Midshipman Lord Louis Mountbatten, became second-in-command
of a little submarine-destroyer, HMS *P31*.

'P' stood for Patrol, and the *P31* was a neat little 650-ton
vessel armed with a single four-inch gun, torpedo-tubes and
– most important – depth-charges for attacking submerged
submarines. 'It is a ripping little ship', his predecessor had
written to him, 'and will suit you down to the ground.
Awfully nice Captain, too.' He was not only nice but away
on other business for most of the time, leaving Mountbatten
in command. 'It was one of the most exciting moments of
my life', Mountbatten exlaimed, 'when I went on-board for
the first time.'

Unfortunately, the war came to an end before he could
accomplish any daring deeds or earn a bravery medal, and in
the sudden rush for economy demanded by the Government,
the *P31* was ordered to be reduced to the level of Care
and Maintenance. With the Captain absent, Mountbatten
decided to postpone this demotion for as long as possible and keep her in full commission in the hope that she
might be included in the Baltic operations then taking place
against the Bolsheviks. At Portland naval base, flanked by
the decommissioned *P30* and *P32*, Mountbatten kept the
little ship in full fighting condition with her crew.

When he learned that the Port Admiral was due to carry out
an inspection, and in fifteen minutes, Mountbatten reacted
calmly, speedily and with characteristic cheek, ordering all
the men except the skeleton Care and Maintenance crew
into a boiler-room. Then he locked the door, suspended a
'Wet Paint' sign on it and went on deck to greet the Admiral
formally.

The Admiral duly arrived, looked around him and commented, 'So your ship is in C and M is it?'

Glancing at his ship's neighbours, Mountbatten assured
him, 'Yes, sir, she's next door to it.'

The *P31* did indeed eventually take part in the Baltic operations, but not with Mountbatten as second-in-command. He
had to be content with a royal inspection and commendation.

When he heard that there was to be a Merchant Navy peace pageant on the Thames at Westminster on 4 August 1919, the fifth anniversary of the start of the war, he contrived to have the *P31* included. Better still, after a word with his cousin Princess Mary, the King and Queen's daughter, it was arranged that they should come on-board as his guests while the boat was moored at Whitehall. He also arranged to have reporters and photographers present, and this mini-event in the brief life of this mini-destroyer was widely reported.

A new captain was appointed to the ship, one who spent more time on-board. Mountbatten did not appear to mind and told his mother that he was 'quite a good sort and does what I tell him, which is the main point'. For his part Lieutenant-Commander T. G. Carter reported that Mountbatten was 'a most zealous and efficient executive officer who has shown much tact in dealing with men'.

Mountbatten needed all the favourable reports he could acquire during 1919 in order to survive in the Royal Navy, which was being cut down to a quarter of its wartime strength. The first young officers to go were those with private means. He did receive a small allowance from his father, but most of the family money had been lost in Germany and Russia. His title once again was a help and a hindrance, but being the King's cousin did usually tilt decisions in his favour, and both his brother George and he survived the freely wielded axe.

The Admiralty was concerned that the young officers who were to remain in the service should complete their education, which had been curtailed by the war, and along with the Duke of York ('Bertie', the future King George VI) and the Duke of Gloucester, Mountbatten went up to Cambridge to study English and French for a few months, though his mind seems to have been occupied mainly with the girls he met.

Mountbatten's education was improved more usefully by two imperial tours which immediately followed his brief time at Cambridge. By pulling hard all the royal ropes he could seize, he managed to get himself appointed an unofficial ADC to his cousin David, the Prince of Wales, who had been asked to tour the Empire as a gesture of thanks for all the support it had given in the recent war. The Prince had already visited Canada, and now faced many months touring the West Indies, Australia and New Zealand, and then India the following year. Dickie provided David with fun and relief from the tedium of meeting boring big-wigs, making speeches, partaking in ceremonials and shaking thousands of hands.

It was at this time that Mountbatten lost his father, whose heart had never recovered fully from the shame and chagrin of losing his post as First Sea Lord. It devastated Mountbatten. 'My admiration and love for him were as high as the sky,' he said. 'He was only sixty-seven. It seemed an awful waste. And considering what he had given to his adopted country, he was treated very shabbily. Churchill's promise that he would be reappointed after the war was broken, and he was never even invited to the surrender of the German fleet – he was just forgotten.'

But Mountbatten at this time also gained a wife. His marriage to the heiress Edwina Ashley, favourite grand-daughter of the mountainously rich Sir Ernest Cassel, was one of the great social events of the period. From living on £300 a year plus his naval pay, Mountbatten was able to buy whatever took his fancy. (Edwina had given him a Silver Ghost Rolls-Royce as a wedding present.)

'Marriage to a very rich woman . . . posed problems,' he accepted. 'I then realised forcibly that the only hope of standing on my own legs was to work. I couldn't hope to produce the money Edwina had. So I had to work very hard in the one profession where money doesn't count. I worked like a beaver to excel. . . . I had to make good *because* I had a rich wife.'

At the time of his marriage, Mountbatten was a full lieu-tenant, still with a need to specialise and make his mark. The world tours with the heir to the throne secured for him numerous valuable connections but did not enhance his professional reputation in the Navy. But Mountbatten had long since mapped out his career, stage by stage, and possessed total confidence that he would achieve his ultimate ambition of becoming First Sea Lord. To do this he must now specialise, and after casting aside his first love, destroyers, and the more exciting submarine and air services, he chose what might appear to be the prosaic branch of signals.

Mountbatten saw signals in the broadest definition, besides the basic ship-to-ship communication. Radio had always fascinated him, and it was at this time rapidly advancing from Morse to voice with the range extending at the same time. It also included, for Mountbatten, the use of movie film for instruction and entertainment in the fleet. His honeymoon had taken in Hollywood, where he had been fired (especially by Charlie Chaplin) with an enthusiasm for shooting and showing film. It lasted for all his life. It was Mountbatten who pushed for a film projector in every ship in the fleet and later founded the Royal Naval Film Corporation.

His career in signals required a two-year course at the Signal School at Portsmouth and later at Greenwich. With the intense concentration he was capable of applying, Mountbatten was able to play plenty of polo, his favourite sport, lead a free-and-easy social life with Edwina, play with their first child, Patricia (now Countess Mountbatten of Burma), and still complete the first part of the course with the highest marks. Even Edwina sometimes wondered how he did it. It puzzled his fellow officers that he somehow managed to lead the life of the complete playboy, then turn up at Portsmouth in his enormous Rolls-Royce (whose radiator mascot was a specially designed representation of a signaller with flags), buckle down to work and beat them all. Not all these contemporaries approved of him, but the authorities were forced to accept that he was brilliant at his job and, at the same time, a first-class teacher.

From 1926 until 1933 Mountbatten served mainly in the Mediterranean, and rose in rank from lieutenant to commander and from assistant fleet wireless and signals officer to the top post of fleet wireless officer. In this role he was responsible for all communications throughout the fleet of some seventy warships, issuing daily news bulletins from the outside world, taking in instructions from the Admiralty, and dealing with any emergency involving ships or individuals.

Mountbatten was one of the most prominent figures in the Mediterranean Fleet not only for his work as head signals officer, but also for the lavish life style enjoyed by Edwina and himself. They had acquired a large villa, entertained royally, drove about Malta in expensive cars and sailed about the coastal waters, and far beyond, in their ocean-going yacht. With his own string of polo ponies, he played hard and intensely so that the competitive element in naval matches increased and some of the light-hearted fun faded proportionately.

In his book *Introduction to Polo*, Mountbatten included this significant piece of advice: 'The primary factor in a successful attack is speed. Generally speaking, if you are the stronger side you will be the attacking side, and it will be to your advantage to speed up the game. . . .' One reason why Mountbatten took his polo so seriously was that he saw the game as a destroyer action in war, something he often dreamed about. The two contests had much else in common besides the speed element: decisiveness yet the lightning ability to switch tactics; individual initiative yet close teamwork; aggressiveness and the ability to shoot straight and fast, if necessary from awkward angles.

Mountbatten organised the filming of his team in action and after the match played it through in slow motion in order to pick out at leisure their mistakes and successes. It might as well have been destroyer exercises. Once, when Andrew Cunningham was Rear-Admiral Destroyers in the Mediterranean, he invited Mountbatten to watch the manoeuvres. 'I watched this absolute wizard handle thirty-six ships entirely by himself,' Mountbatten recalled. '. . . He always saw everything first. . . . It was the greatest one-man performance I have seen on the bridge of a ship.'

In October 1932, Cunningham's superior officer, the C-in-C Mediterranean Fleet, Admiral Sir Ernle Chatfield, wrote of Mountbatten, 'He must not be allowed to confine himself to the Wireless Department any longer.' He had worked his way to the top in this branch, his promotion to commander was imminent, and now – as he had predicted and planned – at the age of thirty-two he was to have command of a destroyer. 'A captain is God almighty,' Mountbatten once said. 'He can do exactly what he wants with his ship. You can make Easter Monday into Good Friday. You can shape the spirit of the ship to your own ideas. You can make yourself hated or loved. And for all this, they pay you – pay you for doing the most wonderful job in the world.'

The ship of which Mountbatten was to be 'God almighty' was the destroyer *Daring* of the 1st Flotilla. HMS *Daring* was brand new, launched in April 1932 and not yet commissioned. Mountbatten, back in England, raced to take a look at her. 'She is even more marvellous than I had imagined possible,' he told his mother exultantly. He had every reason to be excited. She was the last word in destroyer design – 1,375 tons, armed with four 4.7-inch guns and eight torpedo-tubes – and her speed on her trials was 37.9 knots, faster than any other of her class. Like all destroyers of her time, she could be manoeuvred like a motor launch and her acceleration was like that of a car, making it necessary to hold on when she increased speed urgently. To command the *Daring* in the Mediterranean was Mountbatten's dream translated into reality. And to crown his pleasure – his triumph some would say, so competitive was he – he discovered that *Daring* had been the name of the first ever torpedo-boat destroyer to be launched, back in November 1893. Moreover, her speed on her trials had, like his own *Daring*, exceeded that of any other in her class. First and fastest, that's what he liked!

After this satisfactory revelation, Mountbatten seized every book and article on which he could lay his hands in order to become, no less, the world's greatest authority on destroyers. He had plenty of time, for it was another ten months before he took formal command and reported to the Captain (D) of the 1st Flotilla of which he was now a part.

Captain (D) Harold Baillie-Grohman was a fine-looking forty-four year old and an old shipmate of Mountbatten's father. In the First World War he had served under Captain E. R. G. R. Evans and had earned a DSO while operating with the 'Dover Patrol'. Mountbatten liked him and thought him a good flotilla commander, but somewhat lacking in sparkle and positivity. Baillie-Grohman knew Mountbatten by reputation better than Mountbatten knew him, and did not approve of all he had learned. He did not want any showing off and flamboyancy in his Flotilla, nor ostentatious evidence of wealth.

When he was an old admiral, Mountbatten suggested that this writer should go to see him and dig up some memories. 'When he was first appointed to the *Daring*,' Baillie-Grohman recalled, 'I told him, "Look, Dickie, it's all right for you. But please remember in this Flotilla that there's hardly one of us with two brass pennies to rub together. So, be a good chap and watch it." He did, too, he really behaved very well and there was no sign of that early extravagance I had seen when he first came out.'

Perhaps it escaped Baillie-Grohman's notice that the first time Mountbatten gathered his young officers together he told them that he was very rich, lived well and proposed to continue to do so. At the same time he would like them to share his good fortune and a small part of his wealth, and that he would bear all their expenses above their basic mess bills. Not one of them in the least resented the offer.

Mountbatten then cleared the lower deck and made the first of his speeches to the ship's company which were to become a byword in the service. He told them that they were serving in the best ship in the Flotilla, and as soon as the opportunity occurred they were going to win all the prizes. '*Daring* by name, and daring by nature – that's us. And our motto, from that great historian Hakluyt, is to be "We have made every sea the highway of our daring."'

After some preliminary exercises, Baillie-Grohman led the Flotilla out to their base at Malta. Mountbatten had by now got to know his officers and men well, and a number of them related later how swiftly their captain built up the team spirit and somehow gave the impression that they had all known one another for a long time rather than for only a few weeks. They arrived on a Friday, and Mountbatten was looking forward to competitive gunnery drill and working up the following day.

'Unfortunately,' Baillie-Grohman remembered, 'I wasn't able to draw targets on a Friday, so I regretfully made a signal to all my commanding officers, "I know how anxious you all are to get on with working up. You share my disappointment that we shall not be able to do so until Monday. Please inform your ship's company."'

Typically, Mountbatten translated this into more positive language. He told his men:

> We have just reached our destination after seven weeks at sea. The Captain (D) believes that we have now become experienced seamen quicker than any other destroyer in peacetime. Although he is now very anxious to start working up, he has very kindly arranged for us to have a full weekend in harbour to rest and recuperate.

The cheers rang out.

While the men went ashore, Mountbatten had a top-priority task to attend to. He never approved of unnecessary austerity, and although the *Daring* was the fastest and the most modern destroyer in the Royal Navy, he had been shocked to discover that his cabin had no basin with running hot and cold water. He now engaged some Maltese dockyard workmen to fit one. It was not a complicated job, but it required some drilling through a bulkhead and other plumbing operations.

While Mountbatten was ashore and the work was proceeding, Albert Percy Cole, the Head of the Destroyer Section of the Royal Corps of Naval Constructors, happened to pass by the *Daring* and, attracted by the sound of work below, came aboard and investigated. He did not care for what he saw and went at once to the Vice-Admiral Malta's office to report that the structure of the *Daring* was being interfered with. Mountbatten was then summoned and Cole repeated the accusation.

'I lost my temper,' Mountbatten recounted. '"You're a liar. I am doing nothing of the kind and I think it is amazing that you should snoop about in a captain's cabin without permission and then report him for something he has not done."'

The Vice-Admiral ordered Cole to apologise and asked him to leave. 'It was the best thing that ever happened,'

Mountbatten commented surprisingly. 'We became great buddies after this and I had a powerful ally in the Naval Constructors.'

The plumbing was completed in record-breaking time, of course, and the *Daring* was at sea with the rest of the Flotilla at first light on Monday. The first gunnery practice of the 1st Destroyer Flotilla revealed a curious inconsistency in Mountbatten's approach. Since the days of the first torpedo-boats of Yarrow, Thornycroft and White in the 1870s, the essence of these little, black, darting machines was speed – speed of approach, speed of attack and speed of withdrawal. The same applied to the succeeding torpedo-boat destroyers, with their guns as well as torpedo-tubes. The tradition of fast shooting was synonymous with these early boats. Mountbatten, who liked to question and enjoyed exploding axioms, went into the matter carefully. His conclusion was that a lower rate of fire, laying the guns with more precision, would lead to a greater number of hits in any given time. The other Flotilla COs were puzzled when, on this first practice, the *Daring* was clearly firing far fewer shots than they were. They were more surprised when the results were made known, and Mountbatten's ship came out top.

At all other times, Mountbatten added to his reputation for doing everything at the double, and his frequent exploitation of the *Daring*'s speed and manoeuvrability was a wonder to watch. One of his feats was to take his ship up the winding Sliema creek to her moorings going astern at twelve knots, a hair-raising sight which the C-in-C Mediterranean insisted on observing from the *Daring*'s bridge. One slight misjudgment or deviation would have been Mountbatten's undoing. 'I've had some narrow squeaks,' he admitted in a letter home.

PART TWO

THE SHIP

4

The Launch of the *Kelly*

F or reasons known only to the Admiralty, the decision was made that the 1st Flotilla should exchange
ships with some old destroyers on the China Station,
where the threat from a potential enemy appeared much less
than from the Italian fleet in the Mediterranean. Moreover,
the Italians had the fastest cruisers and destroyers in the
world. The whole of Baillie-Grohman's Flotilla was momen-
tarily thrown into a state of depression at the prospect of
losing their spanking new 'D' class ships for 'W' class boats
of the 1914–18 war, which were smaller, slower and in every
particular inferior.

It was December 1934 and a long, hot voyage lay ahead
for the Flotilla, but no CO was more determined to keep up
the spirits of his officers and men than Mountbatten. It was
not only that his competitive spirit was so enormous that he
was determined that his ship should be the happiest and
most efficient. He really felt a tribal, almost a family, loyalty
to his ship's company, and this was strongly reciprocated
although it would have been more difficult to sustain in any
larger class of ship than a destroyer with its complement of
between 175 and 250. Mountbatten soon learnt all of the
names of his ship's company and kept an immaculate card
index on them with any special features and characteristics.

If he learned that there was financial or domestic trouble at the home of an able seaman, this would be entered along with other snippets of news, of the most trivial nature. This enabled Mountbatten to remind the man, perhaps when he was inspecting his gun, of some occasion in the past or make some personal enquiry, creating pride and pleasure.

This written record was supported by Mountbatten's exceptional memory. Once he greeted an ordinary seaman with a noteworthy skill at cards whom he had not seen for some years, 'Grand to see you again, Fred, but your mess will have to be warned before you fleece the lot of them!' Coming from the 'old man' himself, these stories got around in no time.

Mountbatten had been told that they had been assigned the *Wishart*, completed just after the First World War, one of a numerous class built to meet the seemingly limitless demands for destroyers to work with the fleet and fight the U-boats. Most of those which were uncompleted in 1919 were assigned to the scrapyard, like the officers and men to man them. Mountbatten was proud that both he and his new ship had survived.

Everything that could be claimed in favour of the fifteen-year-old *Wishart* was exploited. Mountbatten looked up the records and found that Admiral Sir James Wishart, after whom the ship was named, was an officer under Sir George Rooke and had been appointed C-in-C Mediterranean in 1713. 'A very great and courageous officer.' In fact, Wishart was something of a nonentity, but Mountbatten went one better. At Singapore, after they exchanged ships, he addressed the ship's company:

> We have just left behind a ship with a great name. We have now got the only ship in the Royal Navy with an even greater name. Our new ship is named after the Almighty himself, to whom we pray daily, 'Our Father wishart in heaven.'

That went down very well.

On the voyage west back to the Mediterranean, across the hot Indian Ocean and Red Sea, Mountbatten kept his men busy and happy with competitive games, with prizes, and evening entertainments. 'There was never a dull moment!' Mountbatten saw that a band was formed and himself established a newspaper, *The Wishart News*, carrying items from the outside world as well as the more trivial daily doings of their destroyer.

Mountbatten's matchless ability to create and sustain morale and excellence in all departments was reflected in the reputation of this relatively insignificant, and in many respects obsolete, little ship. It was the first time, at the age of thirty-four, that he was able to prove his powers of leadership. He drove his men hard, discipline was tight at all times, yet the paternal element in his leadership and his irreverent and salty sense of humour were two of the things that kept his ship unusually happy and competitive.

Throughout that summer of 1933 Mountbatten kept up the pressure relentlessly and the *Wishart* was rewarded with top marks in everything against over thirty other destroyers. The ultimate competition had nothing to do with preparing for war, although war with Italy was never far away at this time. It was the annual regatta on 4 September, competed for in heavy whalers. Mountbatten acquired metronomes and installed them in the boats; he worked out a new and ungainly short, sharp stroke that was practised only when out of sight of other competitors and used on the final day with devastating effect. Practice began before 6 a.m. and continued until the men were ready to drop – and did. Practice at cricket and water polo was equally intense, and no coach at the Olympics put in more time at supervising than Mountbatten.

One day Mountbatten told Baillie-Grohman that there was no doubt that the *Wishart* would be outright winner of the regatta – 'Cock of the Fleet', the highest accolade; she would also win the water polo and the cricket. It was a brave prediction. On the day, she swept the board. Baillie-Grohman congratulated him, but Mountbatten was offended that he failed to refer to the prediction. The truth was that his Captain (D) considered Mountbatten brash and over-flamboyant, a spoilt show-off. His superior, Andrew Cunningham, did not share these reservations. 'You had a great victory and it is a great personal triumph,' he told Mountbatten.

The Royal Navy has always been good at spotting talent early, and in spite of Mountbatten's vivid life style ashore with glittering parties for Noël Coward and Hollywood's most glamorous stars of the day, the new Hispano-Suiza car, the yacht and the strings of polo ponies, favourable reports on his professional performance found their way home to the highest officers in the Admiralty.

Early in 1936, his status in the Royal Navy reached a new level. For family reasons, he took leave in London to attend King George v's funeral. Now his cousin and old friend, David, was King-Emperor. At the same time, Mountbatten was summoned to the Admiralty for discussions on the strategy that should be followed in the future, while the threat of war grew in home waters, in the Mediterranean and in the Far East.

The German Navy, reduced to nothing after the great 1919 scuttle and the Versailles Treaty, was again growing in strength. The problem of air-power, and especially the Navy's air-power, was a deep preoccupation of the planning staff. As for Mountbatten himself, he was told that he would be coming to the Admiralty shortly.

On Mountbatten's return to Malta, he was called to a conference of three senior admirals, the C-in-C Admiral Sir William Fisher, his successor designate, Sir Dudley Pound, and Admiral Sir Roger Backhouse, C-in-C Home Fleet and future First Sea Lord. Here he was, then, thirty-five years old and with only three rings on his sleeves, informing the hierarchy of the Royal Navy about his discussions in London with the Prime Minister, the Foreign Secretary and the First Sea Lord. How he revelled in all this top-brass chat, with its implications for his own important future!

Soon after George v's funeral, Mountbatten received his orders to come to the Air Division at the Admiralty. Like everything else, his departure was carefully orchestrated and spectacular. He had made his mark in the Mediterranean and he had to ensure that it was indelible. There are some old sailors alive today who can remember the end of the *Wishart*'s commission and fragments from his speech to his ship's company, which included:

> When we arrived on this station, I said we would win every trophy that was to be won. As you all know the *Wishart* triumphed in every game except football, and in football we lost every match. I feel that I was directly responsible for this because I quite forgot to specify which trophy I meant to win, the silver cup for the best team or the wooden spoon for the worst. We won the spoon so I can safely say that I fulfilled my promise.

After that, he was rowed round the *Wishart* three times by some of the men who had rowed so hard for the regatta that the old destroyer had won in September. Then he was taken ashore, officers and men cheering their hearts out. He took off his cap and waved to them, got into his monster Hispano-Suiza and drove off. But even that was not the end. Before turning for home, he drove to Tigne Point, where he waited to watch his ship leave Valetta harbour and wish her Godspeed on her voyage home.

It was, as Mountbatten described it, a very sentimental moment, but his mind was already on the job ahead. He had been appointed to the Admiralty Air Division at a particularly critical time. With his prophetic eye, he had perceived better than most the implications of future air-power within the context of sea-power. While 'the bomber will always get through' on land, as Stanley Baldwin had proclaimed four years earlier in 1932, Mountbatten was increasingly concerned about the impact of the bomber on the fleet.

The case of bomber-versus-battleship had been argued since the advent of the heavy bomber in the First World War. There were those who believed that the days of the battleship were over, and that control of the sea was dependent on control of the air above it. The Americans and Japanese especially were building up their naval air-power to a high pitch of efficiency. Britain was sadly behind, not only because an influential body of opinion saw air-power as a minor adjunct to the battle fleet, but because of a foolhardy mistake made after the First World War: the Royal Naval Air Service had been handed over to the RAF.

The Smuts Committee in 1917 had recommended the formation of a single air service, the RAF, to take over responsibility for the Fleet Air Arm. While this was modified in 1924, it remained an untidy and inefficient arrangement which left the Fleet Air Arm with obsolete aircraft operating from obsolete carriers. 'I understood better than most of my contemporaries how important it was first to reclaim the Navy's control of its own aircraft and personnel, then to build an efficient and modern Fleet Air Arm as the Americans and Japanese had already done,' said Mountbatten.

The British had created the Japanese air arm after the First World War, just as at the turn of the century they had built her battle fleet, which had beaten first the Chinese and then the Russians. Like his friend Winston Churchill, Mountbatten knew that war was imminent and the modernisation of the Fleet Air Arm was of the utmost importance to the Navy.

From his office at the Admiralty and after extended consultations with senior officers of the Naval Air Division, Mountbatten sent to Churchill, then out of office but at the height of his campaign to awaken the nation to the realities of German aggression, a memorandum on the transfer of naval air-power from the RAF back to its own service.

Churchill, who had been a partner with Mountbatten's father as First Sea Lord in the creation of the original Naval Air Division in 1911–12, took a powerful interest in the recreation of an entirely independent Fleet Air Arm. After reading Mountbatten's memorandum, he gave it to his personal assistant, Desmond Morton, who rewrote it in Churchill's terse style for distribution.

Mountbatten also used his influence with his cousin David, the new King, interesting him in the campaign on behalf of the Navy, and taking along senior officers in the Air Division for talks with him. Against the strong opposition of the RAF, the Navy began at last to make progress in its struggle for control of its own air-power, and won the day finally in

July 1937. But war was too imminent for the completion of all the work that was required for the Navy to create a modern Fleet Air Arm to match those of Japan and the United States.

It is difficult to calculate just how influential Mountbatten was in this reform. There were a number of politicians and naval officers far senior to Mountbatten who shared his views, notably Sir Thomas Inskip, Minister for the Co-ordination of Defence. But with his unique connections, Mountbatten's role was important far beyond what his rank suggested. His had been mainly behind-the-scenes work, but gaining Churchill's active support was a big factor. Anyway, the Board of Admiralty thought highly enough of his contribution to promote him captain in June 1937, the month in which he became thirty-seven himself. It was highly unusual for this rank to be reached by any officer under the age of forty.

The second and equally important campaign Mountbatten fought during his time with the Air Division was for the improvement of defence against enemy air attack, the other side of the naval air factor. Even by the standard of the time, the Navy's ships were severely underequipped with anti-aircraft guns. Long ago Vickers had designed a quick-firing, two-pounder pom-pom gun, which in multiple form – the 'Chicago piano' – was regarded as the one weapon which would always defeat the low-flying bomber, 'hoseing' it out of the sky. Once having discovered this panacea, the Navy relaxed, believing the problem to be solved. Anti-aircraft exercises were usually carried out with towed targets at slow speed, or against 'Queen Bee' pilotless target planes.

All this was far distant from the realities of war, and there was a growing body of opinion in the Navy that the modern high-speed dive- and glide-bomber would make a difficult target for the Vickers gun, which was slow to bear on to the target and slow in rate of fire. Mountbatten was among those most worried about the protection of the Navy's ships against the bomber.

Then, in January 1937, a salesman arrived in Mountbatten's office from the Oerlikon gun works in Zürich. He had a new

20 mm. shell-firing gun with a very high rate of fire and muzzle velocity. The shell was powerful enough to pierce the hull of a submarine and therefore highly lethal against any aircraft.

'I had this man Antoine Gazda in my office at the Admiralty all morning,' Mountbatten recalled, 'trying to shoot him down. I used every argument against his Oerlikon gun, but he shot me down instead. I was then convinced that this was the weapon which could save ships and lives from the low-flying bomber and torpedo-bomber.'

When he witnessed the gun in action, Mountbatten was even more impressed. He got the Director of Naval Ordnance and the Admiralty Controller interested, but there progress halted. It was blocked by the entrenched British gunmakers, notably Vickers, who at that time were almost a branch of the Admiralty. Blocking tactics and procrastination, allied to the age-old naval custom of opposing change, held up the Oerlikon for almost two years. It was not until May 1939 that the Swiss firm received an order for 500 from Britain. Goodness knows how many ships and lives were lost in the opening months of war owing to this delay, and how many ships and lives were saved by its later introduction. The Germans on the other hand knew a good weapon when they saw one and had already ordered thousands. The German quadruple-mounted Oerlikon was a deadly anti-aircraft weapon, as countless Allied pilots (including this writer) learned.

So strong and well-known had his advocacy of the deadly Oerlikon become that there were accusations that Mountbatten had a financial stake in the Swiss firm. One senior officer at the Admiralty scrawled across a memorandum singing the Oerlikon's praises, 'It is quite obvious Captain Mountbatten has an interest in selling this gun.'

Mountbatten's official biographer, Philip Ziegler, has written fairly,

That the Royal Navy would have obtained the Oerlikon gun just as soon without Mountbatten's intervention seems unlikely but cannot be disproved; that they would have got it a great deal earlier if they had heeded his prescience is incontrovertible.

Ziegler did not add that by using his friends in high quarters, Mountbatten succeeded in acquiring for his next ship the first Oerlikons to be delivered.

To have taken a serious part in the recovery of independence of the Navy's Fleet Air Arm, and in the eventual equipping of ships with a considerably strengthened anti-aircraft defence, was an achievement that was reflected in the report on his performance of April 1938. One section of it ran:

> His interests incline mainly towards the material world, and he is, therefore, inclined to be surprised at the unexpected; he has been so successful in that sphere that he does not contemplate failure. His social assets are invaluable in any rank to any service. . . . Desirable as it is to avoid superlatives, he has nearly all the qualities and qualifications for the highest Commands.

In October 1938, the next stage towards these 'highest Commands' was an appointment as Captain (D) of the latest flotilla of destroyers about to emerge from the shipyards. This was a time when appeasement towards Hitler's devilry was in the political air, in Britain and France. Czechoslovakia, Hitler's next intended victim, was being sold out for fear of another world war. The Prime Minister, Neville Chamberlain, had reached an agreement with Germany at Munich and had returned with a piece of paper, which, he claimed, would lead to 'peace in our time'. Mountbatten, with his German background and connections, was among those who knew that appeasement could lead only to further aggression.

On 1 October, Mountbatten's friend and First Lord of the Admiralty, Alfred Duff Cooper, resigned in protest over the shameful Munich agreement. Mountbatten wrote to him that 'I cannot stand by and see someone whom I admire behave in exactly the way I hope I should have the courage to behave if I had been in his shoes, without saying "Well done". . . .'

A few days later, Mountbatten went up to Tyneside, where his Flotilla leader was on the stocks at her builders, Hawthorn, Leslie, and almost ready to be launched. He strongly approved of what he saw. In the same year when Mountbatten had proudly commissioned the *Daring*, the Naval Staff was already considering the next stage in destroyer development. The Germans, French, Japanese and Americans were all building much larger and more heavily gunned ships in this category. The Japanese ships were to carry six five-inch guns and could be regarded as small light-cruisers. The American 'Somers' class had an even heavier armament of eight five-inch guns and no fewer than twelve torpedo-tubes. The French 'Mogador' class, already being commissioned, were of 2,900 tons and were armed with eight 5.5-inch guns. The *Daring*, with her four 4.7-inch, was badly out-gunned by any of these new destroyers.

The British 'Tribal' class, completed in 1938, was intended to meet this gun threat, and Albert Percy Cole was given a requirement of ten 4.7-inch guns, a more modest torpedo armament, a speed of thirty-six knots, all on a displacement of under two thousand tons.

In the event, a compromise had to be made, and only eight twin 4.7-inch guns were mounted; but the 'Tribals' were fine ships which made a great impression. The next stage of development represented a reversion to a smaller displacement, a proportionate reduction in gunpower and an increase in torpedo power. These were the 'J' and 'K' class of 1,700 tons, armed with six twin-mounted 4.7s and ten torpedo-tubes. It is ironic and significant of the reactionary influences still rife among the Naval Staff that one of the thirty-two points in the requirements for these ships was that 'no construction of HA [i.e. high-angle anti-aircraft] fire can be countenanced which might prejudice LA [i.e. low-angle ship-to-ship] performance until such time as aircraft threaten the successful accomplishment of destroyers' main object –

the delivery of torpedo attack . . . 4.7-in. 40° [elevation] at present most suitable'.

Thus, at the same time that Mountbatten's Air Division was fighting for heavier anti-aircraft protection for all HM ships, the Naval Staff was still thinking in terms of a future Battle of Jutland fleet engagement between battleships, without, seemingly, an aircraft in sight. As a result, the 'J's and 'K's were completed with vertical anti-aircraft fire restricted to a four-barrel, two-pounder pom-pom and machine-guns.

Although it had been used experimentally before, Cole adopted the radical (for destroyers) longitudinal system of framing, which gave greater strength to the hull of these vessels. Now a close associate of Cole, Mountbatten strongly approved of this measure, and worked with the architect on a number of aspects of the design of both the 'Tribal' class and the 'J' and 'K' classes.

Mountbatten had for long held the view that the traditional open bridge on destroyers was a poor arrangement. He himself hated to get soaked in any sort of a sea, but he also considered it highly inefficient. He had therefore sat down and designed a bridge which would offer greater protection for the personnel by recessing the fore end and fitting a weather-shield. It was quite simple, but no one had ever considered such an idea before. Cole approved; one was rigged for a 'Tribal' destroyer and it worked like a dream. Mountbatten went on the trials. 'Wonderful ship. My bridge a great success,' he crowed. The captain, the helmsman and others still got wet in heavy seas and at high speeds, but nothing like as wet as they had before.

After this preliminary look over his future ship Mountbatten attended her launch on 25 October 1938. She was to be named *Kelly*, after the late Admiral Sir John Kelly, a more considerable sailor than Admiral Wishart. Kelly had commanded HMS *Dublin* in the Mediterranean in 1914 and was one of the few captains who came out with credit at the time of the abortive pursuit of the *Goeben*. Later, as a rear-admiral, he commanded the 1st Battle-Cruiser Squadron in the North Sea. His daughter Antonia had been persuaded to conduct the launch.

Afterwards, lying in the Tyne, without power or armament, the *Kelly* was already an object of beauty to Mountbatten. 'She had the most beautiful lines of any ship I had seen,' he recalled, although at this stage she was little more than a steel shell. He loved the *Kelly* as if she were his child, and while she was fitting out during the winter of 1938–9 he was constantly going up to Hebburn to supervise her progress. This included his personal comforts, from the fitting of a socket for his electric razor (very advanced in 1938) to the dimensions of his bookshelving, though he was more likely to shave at sea than read a book at sea, or anywhere else for that matter. And this time there was to be no need for makeshift basins with holes rigged through the bulkhead. Mountbatten had had words with King George VI and had volunteered the *Kelly* as temporary royal yacht for his and Queen Elizabeth's state visit to Belgium in September 1939. Mountbatten could therefore give instructions for spacious and luxuriously fitted day and night cabins, and a bathroom fit for a king.

Mountbatten hoped that an old friend and contemporary would come as his first lieutenant, or 'Jimmy-the-One'. He was Lieutenant-Commander Philip 'Egg' Burnett, who received a letter from Mountbatten in June 1938. They met at the shipyard in September, and again at the *Kelly*'s launch on 25 October. Burnett was responsible for the ship's internal economy and organisation, and, on a more specialised level, the *Kelly*'s Asdic, or echo-sounding gear. As the ship approached completion, Mountbatten and Burnett worked together closely and almost feverishly on the detailed layout of storage and accommodation, the provision of a drying-room for the men (Mountbatten was concerned about their comforts, too) and a hundred more points of detail. They exchanged at least one letter a week and met one another once a month, going over the ship together. They also worked throughout closely and harmoniously with the builders, who were used to this co-operation but found these two officers unusually exacting.

An example of this was Mountbatten's fussing about the dimensions of his seat on the bridge. This had to hold him comfortably and be neither too large nor too small, even by half an inch. Like the part-covered Mountbatten bridge, this added to the comfort of the bridge arrangements, something he always favoured, but was also more efficient. It was a warm day when Mountbatten had his first seat fitting, and the Hawthorn, Leslie men were puzzled to see him arriving in a heavy greatcoat as if about to face an Atlantic Force 10 gale. When questioned about this, Mountbatten explained, 'In northern waters one is rarely not wearing a great coat when at sea, and I don't want to be pinched.' No one could remember this sort of provision being made before.

Besides the Mountbatten bridge, the *Kelly* and all the other ships of his Flotilla were fitted with one of his inventions, of which he was inordinately proud, his Station-Keeping Equipment, which facilitated maintaining a steady distance from the next ship when steaming fast in line abreast formation. Other inventions of the past were also incorporated, such as the Mountbatten Ruler and devices to speed up the despatch of signals by semaphore and lamp.

In the early summer of 1939, while Germany denounced the naval agreement with Britain and formed 'the pact of steel' with Italy, Mountbatten began interviewing the officers sent up to Hebburn by the Admiralty for their suitability. 'I was sent up sometime in May,' Lieutenant 'Dusty' Dunsterville recalls. 'I liked him enormously at once and he took me on as signals officer.'

Others selected at this time were Lieutenant Maurice Butler-Bowdon, navigator, Lieutenant Alistair Robin, gunnery lieutenant ('Guns'), Lieutenant-Commander Mike Evans, engineer, and the rest. Over the next three months there was a lot to do. Dunsterville ('Flags') 'got things moved around as I wanted them'. These were not fundamental to the ship's structure, but more for the convenience and efficiency of working, with cupboards and doors in just the right place, the office laid out correctly, and so on. 'The Hebburn people were wonderfully co-operative and a fine lot of men, and we got to know and like them very much.' 'We became great friends all the way down the line', Mountbatten remembered. 'I chummed up with my opposite number, the Managing Director, the First Lieutenant chummed up with the Shipyard Manager, our Engineer Officer with the Engineer Manager of the yard, the Chief Bosun's Mate with the Foreman of Shipwrights, and so on.'

While the officers made a happy ward-room, the *Kelly*, now with boilers and engines fitted, was beginning to assume the familiar configuration of a destroyer for the first time as she lay alongside her jetty. Like an actress painstakingly dressing for the part, she was painted a shining light grey as bright as the brasswork.

Then came the day for her first trials. Still in the hands of her builders, with steam on her boilers and smoke drifting from her single raked funnel, she cast her moorings and edged forward. Her fine stem began to cut delicately through the waters of the Tyne and she turned circumspectly for the open sea for the trials, which were to continue throughout the month of June: speed trials, steering trials, anchor trials, manoeuvring trials, turning trials, full power on one boiler, then four runs over the measured mile, showing an average figure of 34.265 knots, which to Mountbatten's immense satisfaction was faster than any of the other 'K's.

By August there was quite a large naval party on-board for the more warlike trials, of the big guns and the pom-poms, the machine-guns and Lewis guns, the depth-charge launchers and the torpedo-tubes. There were exhaustive inspections of the thousand and more machines and devices; the electrics from lamp signalling to searchlights; the accommodation heaters and radiators to keep the crew warm and the ventilation to keep them cool, the sick-bay, its equipment and drugs; the wireless-room and something very hush-hush and code-named RDF, or radar as it was called after 1943. It was one of the most primitive type, 'borrowed' by Mountbatten from a Navy plane and hoisted on to the foremast, where it looked like a hen-coop. (It was unable to turn independently, so the ship had to turn herself to hold the signal.)

Meanwhile, Mountbatten had also inspected all the other ships of his Flotilla, several of which were behind schedule:

The first torpedo-boat destroyer, HMS *Daring* of 1893. At twenty-seven knots, she was faster than any torpedo-boat, and with the twelve-pounder quick-firer forward and two six-pounders had sufficient gun power to blow one out of the water. Living conditions were rudimentary, allowances generous and discipline less severe than in larger ships.

Mountbatten with his wife's wedding present, a Silver Ghost Rolls-Royce. The signalman mascot was an extra contrived when he chose to specialise in the signals branch.

Baillie-Grohman, Mountbatten's first Captain (D) in the Mediterranean, photographed on promotion to flag rank. He did not entirely approve of Mountbatten's extravagant life style.

HMS *Wishart*, launched in 1919 and already obsolescent when Mountbatten assumed command.

HMS *Daring*, 1932, Mountbatten's first destroyer command, his ambition fulfilled at last. 1,400 tons displacement, she reached almost thirty-eight knots on her trials. Destroyers were now relatively comfortable to serve in, but Mountbatten improved his own comforts further.

A happy gathering of 'The Fighting Fifth' Captains, with Mountbatten himself uncharacteristically camera-shy.

On her trials, the *Kelly* proved herself fastest in her class, to the immense satisfaction of her Captain (D) Lord Louis Mountbatten.

OPPOSITE The launch of HMS *Kelly*, 25 October 1938. She was named after Admiral of the Fleet Sir John Kelly, a hero of the First World War. The displacement of this class had risen to 2,000 tons; primary armament to six 4.7-inch guns, but they could not elevate beyond forty degrees, making them virtually useless against aircraft, the main enemy and cause of her destruction. A single four-inch anti-aircraft gun was later fitted in place of one of her two sets of torpedo-tubes, a belated acknowledgment of the threat from the skies.

Mountbatten on his bridge, 1939.

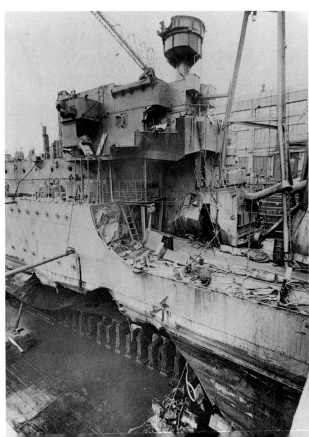

The *Kelly* at the end of her long tow after suffering near-fatal torpedo damage on 9 May 1940, the worst of her numerous mishaps. Then (below) into drydock for examination and repairs. It took only seven months to rebuild her, to the great credit of her builders, Hawthorn, Leslie.

To the chagrin of her regular captain, when Mountbatten temporarily took over HMS *Javelin*, she was unfortunate enough to be torpedoed in the bows and stern simultaneously, leaving only the middle section to be towed home.

December 1940 and the *Kelly* goes to sea again, watched anxiously by some of the company of a sister destroyer.

Andrew Cunningham, the brilliant, modest C-in-C Mediterranean, but not Mountbatten's greatest admirer.

The 'Stringbag', the versatile carrier-borne, torpedo-spotter-reconnaissance Fairey Swordfish, which was delivered to the Fleet Air Arm from early 1936. Much loved by its crews and at first much despised by the enemy, who had to revise their judgment when it crippled the Italian Battle Fleet at Taranto and the giant German battleship *Bismarck* in the Atlantic.

the *Kashmir* and *Kimberley* at Thornycroft's yard, the *Kelvin* at Fairfield's, the *Kipling* at Yarrow's, the *Kingston* at White's, the *Khartoum* at Swan Hunter's and the *Kandahar* at Denny's. He also invited the future Captains, and many other officers, to his house in turn in order to get to know them. There was one exception. His brother Georgie had recently died of cancer, and his son David, now Marquis of Milford Haven, had been appointed to the *Kandahar*.

Down at Chatham Barracks, the Victorian 'stone' ship, where long lists of names were to be found at any time outside the drafting office, the draft chits were going out for a ship up on the Tyne that no one had ever heard of. Within a day or two a hundred or so seamen, some still raw from civilian life, had taken the long train ride north and, with kitbag on shoulder, had headed for the Hebburn yard of Hawthorn, Leslie.

One of them recalled that day in August 1939:

> Went up to Hebburn with the Steaming Party and on turning to, met the Chief Gunner's Mate, Tusky Hales, just one of the many gentleman I was to serve with. He introduced me to the Buffer and Coxswain, after which I met Lieutenant-Commander Burnett and the Navigator Lieutenant Butler-Bowdon. I was to be QM [Quartermaster], being the oldest, I was to get things organised. That night we made the first of what was to be many visits to the 'Commercial' [public house].

Towards the end of August the last of this first intake of the *Kelly*'s company had reported for duty. Without exception, cynical old veterans and raw youngsters alike, they knew that this was going to be no ordinary commission, and their captain no ordinary captain. For one thing, every one of them had been called to Mountbatten's day cabin immediately after coming on-board, to be sized up and chatted to. He appeared to know a surprising amount about them already, and asked a number of questions before standing up from his desk and shaking the sailor by the hand, an extraordinary experience. 'I mean to say,' they would write home, 'he is a famous Lord and the King's cousin.'

The *Kelly*'s acceptance trials were completed before the last week in August, as the days of peace ran out. There was not a family in Britain that did not suspect that another war with Germany was a few weeks or days away. Down in the engine-room the sailors took over from the professional dockyard men, who gave them last tips before shaking hands with wishes of good luck.

More farewells and good wishes were being exchanged in Mountbatten's cabin, with mutual affection and respect and necessarily with some formality. One written statement was signed by the Hawthorn, Leslie representative:

We, Messrs Hawthorn, Leslie & Co. Ltd, Hebburn-on-Tyne, at/off The Tyne handed over this twenty-third day of August, one thousand nine hundred and thirty-nine, at 3.30 p.m. o'clock, HMS *Kelly*, constructed by us for His Majesty's Navy.

The other, which Mountbatten signed as 'Louis Mountbatten, Captain, Royal Navy,' read:

Received from Messrs Hawthorn, Leslie & Co. Ltd, Hebburn-on-Tyne, HMS *Kelly*, this twenty-third day of August, one thousand nine hundred and thirty-nine, without prejudice to outstanding liabilities.

Some of the officers of HMS *Kelly*'s first commission.

Without ceremony or solemnity, the Red Ensign was hauled down and the White Ensign broken aboard. The Royal Navy had a new fighting ship, which had cost the taxpayer £392,226, or just short of £10 million in present-day money. World war was eleven days away.

Just as in 1914, the Navy called up the Reserve Fleet and every fighting ship put to sea, supposedly for exercises but in reality to be ready for a surprise enemy attack. The *Kelly* put to sea, too, but for the present her fighting value was nil, being without so much as a single round of machine-gun ammunition. By 25 August she had reached the Thames estuary, and that afternoon berthed in Chatham.

After the relative peace and tranquillity of the Tyne, Chatham was in a state of hectic activity, with every kind and size of vessel on the move, or taking in stores, refuelling or painting ship. Within a few minutes the *Kelly* had lighters alongside and the remainder of the ship's company was marched from their barracks and on-board. Mountbatten cleared the lower deck aft and faced all 230 officers, petty officers and men for the first time. For no more than a second or two he cast his eyes over them, and liked what he saw, though some looked pathetically young and no doubt one or two of the older hands who were still ordinary seamen might give some trouble.

As for the men, they recognised that, without qualification, their captain was a man of exceptional substance, charisma and style, who would not for one moment allow anyone to pull a fast one on him; and, with his title and reputation, he was also a bit awesome. When he spoke, his voice was firm and decisive. He began:

In my experience, I have always found that you cannot have an efficient ship unless you have a happy ship, and you cannot have a happy ship unless you have an efficient ship. That is the way I intend to start this commission, and that is the way I intend to go on – with a happy and an efficient ship.

We have come to Chatham to store and ammunition ship. Now, normally we are allowed three weeks by the Admiralty to complete this operation. I have decided that it must be completed in three days. I expect you all to play your part irrespective of whether you are a stoker or a seaman, a writer or a cook. The motto of this ship is "Keep On". Now we have a job to do. Let's do it.

The petty officers took over, assigning the men to their jobs, and within ten minutes the loading work had started: sides of beef, fresh vegetables, sacks of flour and countless crates of cans for the victualling stores; ropes and blankets; torpedoes; two-pounder pom-pom ammunition and 4.7-inch shells (250 rounds per gun). Every hour there was a brief pause for tea, and supper was taken in rotation like sleep through the night, so that the work never ceased. It was the same all through the next day and the day after that, while empty lighters were replaced by loaded lighters until it seemed as if this small man o'war could contain nothing more. Some of the young lads had to be given breaks, some of the old hands grumbled, but somehow the spirit was sustained. The fact that the officers had stripped down and were working with the men was a strong reason for that. It was like coaling ship in the old days, when everyone but the captain and surgeon took part.

They completed the work within the permitted three days and nights, and the petty officers passed on the word of thanks from Mountbatten. Then there was shore leave for a few hours for most of the men. One of them recorded:

We strutted round Chatham with our tiddly cap badges, HMS *Kelly*, visited all the local pubs, chatted the barmaids up, saluted the Captain as he passed in his chauffeur-driven Rolls with a silver signalman as the mascot. Don't know why we felt so happy, but we did.

Then, it was back on-board: 'We are sailing for Portland within the hour.'

That night, 29–30 August, when the last hopes for peace were dying, the *Kelly* steamed down Channel, in full moonlight within sight of the twinkling resorts of Bexhill, Eastbourne and Brighton, where the lights would soon go out for almost six years.

The working-up trials began at once after they reached Portland, for whatever the individual qualities of the officers and men, they had not yet worked together as a team. Some of them had not even learned how to find their way about below decks. In peacetime, they would have had three months; now they had scarcely three days.

Mountbatten took them to sea, liaising with the RAF, who laid on a towed target with a drogue for the anti-aircraft guns. The multiple pom-pom opened up with a devastating row, the .5s, Lewis and machine-guns providing a background chorus. Empty shell cases rattled on the deck and the ship was filled with the stench of spent cordite. One pom-pom shell hit and severed the towing-wire, and the drogue fell limply into the sea. A party of stokers off watch and on deck let out a cheer, and one of them called, 'Why should England tremble when old Stripey's behind the gun!'

Then the main armament opened up at the distant sea targets, and the *Kelly* flinched at the recoil and the savage crack of the 4.7s. Neatly stowed gear below was hurled to the deck. In the forward mess-deck, a bag of flour fell from a shelf and burst on the ship's cat, Hawthorn (after the builders), who anyway did not care for all the noise.

Added reality to the gunnery trials was provided by the signal they took in before returning to Portland: 'General from Admiralty. Fuse all shell, ship all warheads.'

They were in port on Sunday 3 September. In the morning, Mountbatten was lecturing his men on his Station-Keeping Equipment. 'Now I have given you the basic principles of operating my gear,' he was concluding. 'If war at this moment breaks out, you know enough about it to work it . . .' Mountbatten was such a good actor that he deserved all the luck he seemed to receive, and today he had it. A rating appeared and handed him a piece of paper. Mountbatten paused to read it and then announced, 'Well, war has at this moment broken out.'

Back in his cabin, Mountbatten read the latest signal:

'From Admiralty to all concerned at home and abroad. Most immediate. Commence hostilities at once with Germany.'

The message had already raced round the ship. Mountbatten now followed it up with a Tannoy message after the 'still' had been piped:

There is no need for me to tell you what you already know, but one thing I will tell you. When we leave the shelter of this harbour we shall be right in the face of the enemy, who will be out to destroy us. We must therefore find him and destroy him first.

Mountbatten recalled that time when he had been alone with his father twenty-five years earlier, dining in the Admiralty, the crowds outside cheering on their way to the Palace. This time it was a more solemn and fearful occasion. To his wife Edwina he wrote that night: 'So the war has started with all its horrors and destruction. In August 1914 I was thrilled, excited and pleased – now I have a home and family to think of and I'm worried.'

5

'I was really hopping mad over this'

LIEUTENANT DUNSTERVILLE

They called it 'crab fat', the oily, heavy, drab-grey paint created for RN ships in time of war. It was not strictly speaking camouflage paint, though it blended in well with the grey northern seas. It was Home Fleet paint intended to cover the gleam of peacetime sheen, which had been so proudly applied by Hawthorn, Leslie up at Hebburn only a few weeks earlier. And now, immediately after Prime Minister Neville Chamberlain had completed his mournful speech announcing that a state of war existed between Germany and Britain and her Empire, every member of the *Kelly*'s company was told off to paint the ship. It was a miserable job at the best of times, but it seemed like desecration to 'crab fat' their shining new destroyer.

From stages and boats, the men in overalls slapped on the paint with big, round brushes, covering the hull, the upper works, the gun turrets and the gun barrels, too, to the chagrin of Alistair Robin. Mountbatten himself worked from a catamaran with Petty Officer Clarke and two seamen, his overalls soon no longer laundry white. It was a fine day with high, scattered cloud. The air-raid sirens had gone off in London and south-east England, they had learned, but it had been a false alarm. The only other sign of war at Portland was the balloons which had already arisen above this naval base as some sort of protection against low-flying enemy aircraft.

When their painting was finished, shore leave was piped for most of the crew and a great deal of beer was downed at the White Ensign Club. There was much jokey, defiant talk about Hitler and the German Navy, and not a word about the flutters of unease that everyone felt in one degree or another. Somewhere out there, under the sea, on the surface or in the air above, an enemy intended to kill you, and however courageous you prided yourself on being, this was a very different condition from what had prevailed a few hours earlier. And even if – as some were saying – it would all be over by Christmas, this new state of affairs would exist tomorrow and the next day.

Mountbatten told them the following morning, 'We are going out for anti-submarine exercises. We may meet the real thing. Lookouts will be posted, and I shall deal severely with anyone who does not keep a proper lookout.' The warning was justified. The Germans had despatched almost their entire strength of U-boats, twenty-one in all, to patrol British waters. Already on the previous day the liner *Athenia* had been torpedoed and sunk. There were children and Americans among the drowned.

For the first time, the *Kelly* sailed in company, with another destroyer, the *Acheron*, and a small anti-submarine motor-boat. Within the hour the three boats were in an emergency. Someone in the motor-boat thought he saw torpedoes approaching the *Kelly* and transmitted a warning. Mountbatten ordered a sharp turn to comb their tracks. Nothing was seen, but almost at once 'Egg' Burnett reported a 'ping' on his Asdic, and Mountbatten ordered a pattern of depth-charges to be launched. The *Acheron*, astern, did the same, and the sea suddenly erupted with a dozen explosions at varying depths, sending up great spouts of white water, just as if they were being dive-bombed. Both destroyers then turned sixteen points and steamed at low speed through the area, searching for signs of wreckage. Mountbatten thought he saw an oil slick and even ordered a sample to be taken. The only certain victims were the fish which floated to the surface, dead or stunned in great numbers. Hooks were lowered to bring in several fine big fish, and in many messes that night the cooks served up top quality cod.

Mountbatten, lusting for success for his ship and himself, optimistically claimed a 'probable' U-boat kill. 'When we heard this,' an officer in the Naval Intelligence Division at the Admiralty recalled, 'we burst out laughing. We knew that there wasn't a U-boat within a hundred miles, but it was typical of the man.'

The *Kelly*'s daily newspaper, edited by Bob Knight, took a more hopeful view:

We all hope that the *Kelly*'s and *Acheron*'s efforts did away with one of the pests that sank, without warning, the liner *Athenia*. . . . There is plenty of corroborative evidence to show that there were two U-boats here yesterday – one in Weymouth Bay and one in West Bay . . . to be missed by one submarine and bag another all in the first day of war is good going.

A more serious note was struck, in capital letters, by the following instructions: 'WHENEVER ANYBODY SEES A PERISCOPE OR TORPEDO TRACK THEY MUST DRAW THE BRIDGE'S ATTENTION TO THIS AT ONCE, EVEN IF IT MEANS YELLING AND SCREAMING THE PLACE DOWN.'

In those first days of war, the *Kelly* was working up more successfully in happiness than in efficiency, and it would be some time before Mountbatten was satisfied on both counts. He pressed ahead with the ship's training programme. 'The RAF was having a quiet time of it,' he recalled. 'And nothing much was happening for the Army. It might be what came to be known as the "phoney war" for them, but it was real war from the very start for the Navy. So you can see why I was so keen to have my ship ready to take part. There was only one brief interruption to my programme.'

Mountbatten was referring to a royal duty he had to fulfil

little more than a week after the outbreak of war. Winston Churchill, First Lord of the Admiralty again, summoned Mountbatten to London on 10 September. They were old friends and the processes of thought of the two men often ran in parallel. 'We have to bring the Duke and Duchess of Windsor home from France, Dickie. Would you mind doing the job?'

This did not take Mountbatten entirely by surprise. He was privy to Palace goings-on and knew that it had been regretfully concluded by George VI and Queen Elizabeth that the ex-King and his wife must be brought back to England, which they had not been allowed to visit since Edward VIII's abdication. Churchill had eagerly volunteered to organise the travel arrangements.

Mountbatten agreed at once. So the warship intended to take the present King and his consort to Belgium that same month on a state visit would be used instead to bring back the banished ex-King and his twice-divorced wife. It was fortuitous that the luxurious royal suite had not been removed. Mountbatten was told that detailed instructions would follow, and he returned to Portland.

Mountbatten was under the impression that strict security prevailed about this mission, but a news item in the *Daily Mirror*, which he did not see, suggested that a new fast destroyer would be embarking the Duke and Duchess and the *Kelly*'s men put two and two together very easily. So, when orders were received on Monday 11 September to raise full steam by 11 a.m., everyone knew that they were off to France and that training would be suspended for a day or two. Confirmation arrived in the form of Randolph Churchill, Winston's son, dressed in the uniform of his regiment, the 4th Hussars. He had been sent to add gravitas to the occasion, but actually appeared to be rather drunk. Also he had put his spurs on back to front. When at the last minute Mountbatten himself was piped on-board, he noticed this gaffe but said nothing.

'Egg' Burnett greeted his Captain: 'The men tell me we're going to France to pick up the Duke and Duchess of Windsor. Is that true?'

Mountbatten looked rather shocked at this apparent breach of security. 'How did they know?'

'I think they read it in the newspapers, sir.'

Mountbatten ordered the lower deck to be cleared and told his men, 'We are about to embark on what I understood was a secret mission.' He smiled and continued, 'It still remains an important mission. In a few minutes we leave for Cherbourg at high speed. Our passengers will be treated with all the respect and ceremony due to the Royal Family but I think you'll see very little of them.'

Later, Mountbatten had a few private words with his officers. To them, his tone was somewhat different: 'I don't want you to be over-impressed by the Duke and Duchess's charm.' 'Dusty' Dunsterville said later that he thought that they might be seduced into thinking that the wrong brother was King.

The *Kelly* reached Cherbourg late in the afternoon after a swift, safe passage, and Mountbatten made his way ashore with Randolph Churchill to the Admiral Commandant's house. There he greeted his cousin, the man he had once described as 'my best friend'. They had only just arrived after a long and anxious road journey from the Côte d'Azur. Wallis appeared fretful about her luggage and her three cairn terriers, Pookie, Prisie and Dette.

The ex-King and Randolph had known one another since childhood, too. The Duke laughed after they shook hands and pointed at Randolph's spurs: 'They're on back to front, Randolph.' Churchill's son could only laugh and apologise for this gaffe. Mountbatten was delighted that he had mischievously left the correction to the Duke.

'When will you be ready to leave?' Mountbatten asked him.

'Just as soon as our things are stowed.'

'Good, where are they?'

The Duke waved a hand towards the piles of suitcases and boxes stacked on the Admiral's lawn.

Mountbatten exclaimed, 'Do you mean to tell me that those things are yours?'

'They certainly are, Dickie.'

'But you're to be piped aboard. I can't have you piped aboard with all those cardboard boxes.'

The Duchess intervened, politely but firmly. 'Well, Dickie, just because we're the first refugees you have seen is no reason for the Royal Navy to turn up its nose at us. These are my clothes and David's things. You can arrange it any way you want – take David out first and then, when nobody's looking, send the launch back for me. But these things go with us.'

Mountbatten reluctantly agreed. He had to.

It was dusk when the *Kelly* steamed out of Cherbourg harbour, at once tucking in her bows and accelerating to thirty knots. Supper had been laid in the day cabin, and Mountbatten left the bridge to join his passengers. The Duchess was looking about her, at the fine panelling, the deep-pile carpet and comfortable sofa and chairs. 'You do yourself very nicely, Dickie,' she said. 'I never knew destroyers could be so comfortable.'

Mountbatten laughed and explained the reason. A steward offered Randolph another whisky, and they began supper. Mountbatten soon left them, and Randolph and David later followed him up to the bridge. Here David stood beside Butler-Bowdon and subjected him to a series of ridiculous questions like, 'Where are we, pilot?', 'How do you know?' and 'But how do you know which buoy it was?'

It was a calm, black night and, to the relief of all the bridge personnel, the Duke returned to the cabin. Before they entered Portsmouth harbour, he again expressed his anxieties about their reception. 'I don't know how this will work out,' he said. 'War should bring families together, even a royal family. But I don't know.' He pressed the Duchess's hand, turned and made his way up to the bridge again as they entered the harbour.

In pitch darkness, the *Kelly* was brought alongside Farewell Jetty, the very jetty from which the Duke of Windsor had embarked after his abdication. As soon as they were secured, a single light was switched on, revealing a shadowy reception party, a red carpet from the bottom of the gangway, the dark shape of a limousine. The Duke and Duchess stepped on to the gangway and the lights were switched on above them, revealing the bayonets of the guard of honour, at attention, with the band playing (not altogether appropriately) 'God Save the King'.

At the base of the gangway, they turned and looked up at their rescue vessel, with Mountbatten visible on the bridge, the men lined up along the rail. In turn the Duke and Duchess called out their thanks, the Duke adding, 'God speed in the months that lie ahead.'

'War should bring families together,' the Duke had said. There was no sign of this happening at Portsmouth that night. The laying on of the *Kelly*, the warm reception at Portsmouth and the limousine to take them away were all organised by Churchill. There was no representative of the Royal Family present, no message of welcome – nothing. Their shelter for the night was to be Admiralty House. Here the C-in-C Portsmouth and his wife gave them a cordial welcome and a light supper. He was Admiral Sir William 'Bubbles' James, who as a child had been the model for Millais's famous portrait advertisement for Pears soap, and his wife Dorothy 'dispensed the warmest hospitality'.

While this exalted foursome made polite conversation in the Admiralty House drawing-room, most of the *Kelly*'s crew were given leave until midnight and a number of 'Pompey' pubs offered them excellent hospitality, too, though for cash.

Before dawn on 13 September, the *Kelly* was on the move again, out past the Needles and west along the southern coast of England, the beautiful coastline of Dorset and Devon, past Drake's Island off Plymouth, and up the Hamoaze into Devonport naval base.

The war had run for only two weeks, but the German armies had already conquered half of Poland and the Russians were about to invade that unhappy country from the east. Most of the British Expeditionary Force had arrived in France along with RAF units to support them. At Devonport, with the arrival of other 'K' ships, Mountbatten began to form his 5th Flotilla, inevitably to be known (on his instructions) as 'The Fighting Fifth'. Still inexperienced, but with great enthusiasm, his destroyers began hunting the seas for U-boats. This was part of Churchill's policy. Always eager for taking the offensive and finding a defensive role anathema, he even employed carriers in hunting groups to scour the seas for the enemy.

This was all contrary to the lessons learned in the last U-boat war. The oceans are too vast to hunt U-boats. The most effective method of minimising losses, it had been expensively discovered, was to protect convoys as strongly as possible and (when available) with air-cover, await the arrival of the enemy and then attack. At the time of the *Kelly*'s return to Devonport, the U-39 attacked one of these hunting groups. Her torpedoes just missed the *Ark Royal*, the only modern aircraft carrier in commission. The counter-attack by the *Ark Royal*'s destroyers blew the U-boat to the surface and sank her.

A few days later another hunting group, based round the carrier *Courageous*, was shadowed by another U-boat. While two of her escorting destroyers were away pursuing a third U-boat, U-29 caught the carrier as she was about to land on some of her aircraft. Two of three torpedoes struck her. She was an old, lightly armoured vessel and she began to sink at once.

The *Courageous*'s SOS was taken in by the *Kelly*, and Mountbatten ordered full speed to the scene, forty miles distant. The weather was running half a gale and their little ship was battered about as never before, but in just over an hour they saw lights ahead. They came from two neutral liners which were doing what they could to pick up survivors; there were destroyers at work, too. The seas were running high and the area was covered with debris, oil and aviation fuel. It seemed impossible that anyone had survived, but the American liner had picked up forty or so of the *Courageous*'s men.

At great risk, the *Kelly* launched a boat and drew alongside the towering hull of the liner, and one by one took off the men, all oil saturated and many badly injured. For two hours the survivors were ferried and brought on-board the destroyer. The youngsters particularly among the *Kelly*'s

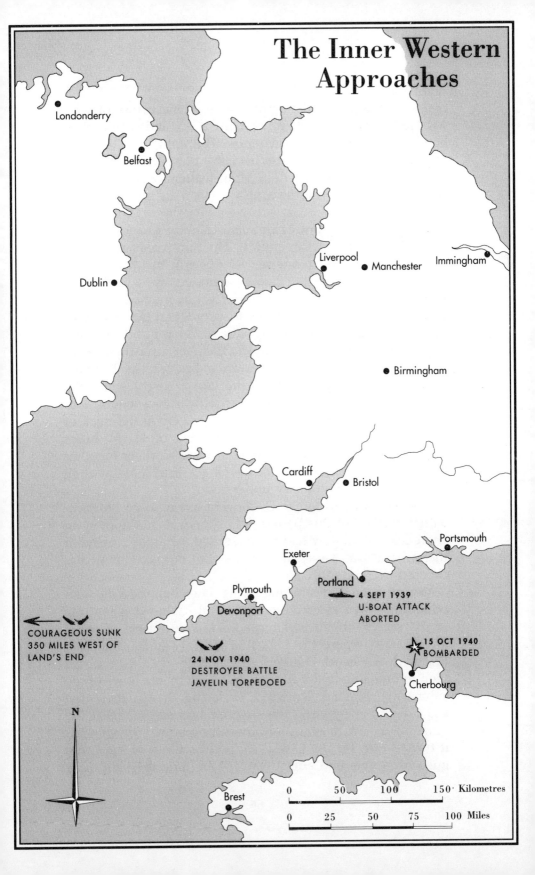

The Inner Western Approaches

Londonderry

Belfast

Dublin

Liverpool • Manchester

Immingham

Birmingham

Cardiff • Bristol

Portsmouth

Exeter

Portland

Plymouth

Devonport

4 SEPT 1939
U-BOAT ATTACK
ABORTED

← COURAGEOUS SUNK
350 MILES WEST OF
LAND'S END

24 NOV 1940
DESTROYER BATTLE
JAVELIN TORPEDOED

15 OCT 1940
BOMBARDED

Cherbourg

N

Brest

| 0 | 50 | 100 | 150 Kilometres |

| 0 | 25 | 50 | 75 | 100 Miles |

crew were appalled at this first sight of the reality of war, with men thick with oil and choking it up, and with broken bones and bleeding from wounds. The Captain of the *Courageous* had gone down with his ship, but her Commander, Connolly Abel Smith, whom Mountbatten knew well – he was a naval equerry to the King – was among those dragged on-board.

There was a long line of ambulances at the quayside when the *Kelly* docked at Devonport. The survivors who could walk were escorted tenderly, wrapped in blankets, down the gangway, while the badly wounded were carried on stretchers. U-boat warfare was not yet as intense as it was to become, and had been back in 1917 when the campaign came close to cutting off supplies to Britain and bringing her to her knees. But already by October 1939 there were serious losses among merchantmen besides the U-boats' major successes against the Navy, the *Courageous* and the battleship *Royal Oak* in the supposedly safe anchorage of Scapa Flow. Mountbatten and his men were in the thick of the campaign in the Western Approaches, on escort duties and with hunting groups. The men were working together better, and the importance of keeping a strict lookout at all times was now thoroughly understood.

'We were in and out of Devonport like a yo-yo,' Mountbatten recalled of this period. 'No sooner were the men on shore leave than they had to be recalled, from the cinema or the pubs. It was pretty tiring work. But our second success cheered everyone up.'

Mountbatten was referring to the day when the *Kelly* with other ships was escorting a convoy up-Channel when one of the merchantmen was torpedoed. The escorts all raced for the area where the U-boat was likely to be, the *Kelly* first with her depth-charges. After a second attack, oil was seen to be rising to the surface, followed by the bows of the submarine, like a killer whale surfacing. It was their first sight of the enemy and the surprise was so great that the guns were slow to bear on to the sitting target; too slow, as it turned out, for the U-boat slipped back out of sight in a gush of spume and angry water. This time they felt quite safe in claiming a certain 'kill' and did so. But, though badly shaken, the enemy had escaped.

On 20 October 1939, the 5th Flotilla was suddenly ordered north, and their work in the Western Approaches abruptly ceased. The Flotilla now consisted of three 'K's, the *Kelly*, *Kingston* and *Kandahar*, although the other two ships were not yet fully worked up. It was for this reason that only the *Kelly* was diverted to an urgent operation even before the Flotilla reached Scapa Flow.

Besides their U-boats the Germans were having some success with their surface raiders. The pocket battleship *Deutschland* had sunk a number of merchantmen in the Atlantic, after punctiliously taking on-board the crews. She also captured the British freighter *City of Flint* and put a prize crew on-board, together with some six hundred of these other captured crews. Then she was ordered to attempt the journey to Germany. The *Kelly*, among several other warships, was ordered to intercept and capture the *City of Flint*, but by this time she had reached the Norwegian coast and was working her way south along the 'Indreled'. This was the route through the maze of islands and channels stretching for many hundreds of miles and almost all the way within Norwegian territorial waters.

This was just the sort of task, with a touch of Sir Francis Drake to it, that Mountbatten relished. He raced across the North Sea, hell-bent on being first and bringing fame to his ship and almost certainly winning a DSO for himself. On reaching the Norwegian coast they were at once intercepted by a patrolling Norwegian gunboat. The *Kelly* was ordered out of Norwegian waters, and Mountbatten at once complied. But while doing so, he could not resist calling out in German through his loudhailer, 'Please give my compliments to my cousin, Crown Prince Olaf.' 'Typical Lord Louis!' was the approving comment of his men.

After all this fast cruising, the *Kelly* was low in fuel and Mountbatten had to replenish her tanks before continuing the hunt. When they did so, Dunsterville and Butler-Bowdon judged that they were heading for a part of the coast which the *City of Flint* must already have passed. Mountbatten pooh-poohed their opinion and they remained on course, finally missing any possibility of an interception. Mountbatten was furious, but he had the good grace to apologise for his mistake to his two officers.

'I really was hopping mad over this,' Dunsterville recalled. 'We could have got them no trouble at all and freed 600 seamen instead of leaving them as prisoners of war for five years. It is absolutely basic that in any intercepting situation like this you go to the position furthest on your target could have reached, and then work back. But Mountbatten would have none of this. He wanted to catch the ship first and at once, to make a splash. In spite of wartime he still thought of making a splash first instead of viewing the sober merits of the case.'

The *Kelly* then headed back to Scapa Flow to continue her duties at high speed – too high speed for the heavy weather, thought some. And they were proved right. At twenty-eight knots, she was hit by a huge wave, which rolled her over to fifty degrees on her starboard side, carrying away her guardrails, boats and davits, along with an off-watch stoker who was never seen again. A destroyer had never been known to survive a roll as violent as this, and later Mountbatten wrote to A. P. Cole to congratulate him and to explain the circumstances. On the other hand it would have been hard to find a destroyer commander who would have maintained such a high speed in such hostile conditions.

The incident marked the beginning of the series of misfortunes to the *Kelly* to which, on every occasion, Mountbatten himself contributed to some degree. This state of affairs was so notorious that it became a legend in the Navy, leading to sardonic sayings like, 'There's no one anyone would sooner be in a tight corner with than Dickie Mountbatten, and no one capable of getting you into one quicker.' When Mountbatten was later appointed captain of a large aircraft carrier, George VI was heard to remark sadly, 'Poor old *Illustrious!*'

The damage to the upper works on this occasion made it necessary for Mountbatten to take the *Kelly* back to her builders for repairs. At the same time, she was given special

strengthening on her bottom against ice for possible partici-
pation in Churchill's plan, 'Operation Catherine', for a naval
force to penetrate the Baltic in March 1940 and attack and
neutralise the German Navy. (It never took place.)

A new sinister figure, and a new equally sinister weapon,
now influenced the career of the *Kelly*. 'Lord Haw-Haw', the
Irishman William Joyce, had for some weeks been broadcast-
ing demoralising news to the British people from Berlin.*
Some of the claims about Allied losses were absurd, but from
others it was clear that he was privy to German intelligence
to a disturbing degree. For example, he made claims triumphantly and with some accuracy about the German magnetic
mine, which had already sunk a large number of ships. They
were usually dropped by German aircraft in coastal waters,
harbour mouths and river estuaries, and were activated not
by contact but magnetically by the proximity of a ship, and
could not be swept by orthodox methods.

On the evening before the *Kelly* was due to sail again, her
repairs complete, a number of her sailors were listening, as
usual, to the regular broadcast of Lord Haw-Haw, which
usually gave everyone some innocent fun. It certainly did
that night. 'And where is your Lord Louis Mountbatten?' he
demanded in his familiar oily voice. 'You mustn't imagine
we don't know. We do. He is on the Tyne. But he will never
leave it.'

This was considered a great joke. Mountbatten was already
on-board, and they would be going down river, in company
with another destroyer, HMS *Mohawk*, the next morning.
'Farewells' and 'Godspeeds' were being exchanged with the
Hawthorn, Leslie men, who by now were almost as closely
associated with the *Kelly* as the ship's company. At that
moment an urgent signal was taken in: 'Two oil tankers in
trouble position 155 degrees 05 minutes north, 001 degrees
07 minutes west. U-boats believed in area. Proceed to area
and intercept.'

The *Kelly* cast off, and Mountbatten ordered a speed far
in excess of what was prudent for the tricky Tyne, and

* He was hanged after the war.

certainly took no regard for other shipping. She got as far
as Jarrow Staithes safely, when a large merchantman hove
into sight, navigating quite properly. Mountbatten ordered
full astern, and it was as well that his destroyer's stopping
power was as spectacular as her acceleration. In a cauldron
of churned white water from the reversing propellers, the
Kelly began to go astern just in time. Then she was off
again, past the breakwater at Shields and out into the open
sea.

It was 4 p.m. in murky December light before Mountbatten
sighted one of the damaged tankers, the *Athol Templar*. She
was on fire and clearly sinking, and Mountbatten signalled
that he would be coming alongside to take off survivors.
Before he could do so, now proceeding at low speed, he
became aware of a curious bumping beneath his ship's
keel, as if they had struck a reef. Everyone on-board felt
it, those on the lower deck most violently. Some thought
that they were feeling the shock of the nearby *Mohawk*
dropping depth-charges. Then, right aft, there was a tremendous explosion. They had struck a mine, just like the
two tankers, but by incredible luck it had been a faulty
magnetic mine and had not exploded on proximity or even
first contact, when it would have blown the bottom out of
the ship.

Everyone was thrown to the deck by the shock, and there
were many bruises and cuts, but nothing worse. The *Kelly*
lay wallowing in the rollers, helpless to pick up any of
the tanker's crew – most were recovered by the *Mohawk* –
and with propellers so damaged that she could only await
a tow. There was water in the tiller flat, and men were
ordered down there to recover the gear and prop up the
bulkheads. Darkness had fallen, and the *Kelly*'s men remembered Lord Haw-Haw's threat: not such a hollow one this
time.

As they were towed painfully back to the Hawthorn, Leslie
yard, Mountbatten had brought before him a young stoker
for whom the ordeal had proved too much. He had 'deserted
his post in face of the enemy'. With engines closed down,
there was only the faint sound of water against the hull

when the young stoker was escorted into Mountbatten's cabin.

'Do you know the penalty for this offence?' Mountbatten demanded.

The white-faced sailor, at attention, cap in hand, answered quietly, 'Yes, sir. Death.'

'Good,' said Mountbatten. 'I shall stand this case over and deal with it later.'

He dealt with it in an interesting and characteristic way. Two hours later, as they approached the Tyne estuary, he cleared the lower deck and spoke to the ship's company:

Today we have been through one of the most trying experiences which can befall a newly commissioned ship in war [he began]. Out of 240 men on-board this ship, 239 behaved as they ought to have, and as I expected them to behave, but one was unable to control himself and deserted his post, and incidentally his comrades in the engine-room. I had him brought before me a couple of hours ago, and he himself informed me that he knew the punishment for desertion of his post could be death. You will therefore be surprised to know that I propose to let him off with a caution, one caution to him and a second one to myself for having failed in four months to impress my personality and doctrine on each and all of you to prevent such an incident from occurring. From now on I will try to make it clear that I expect everyone to behave in the way the 239 did, and to stick to their post in action to the last. I will under no circumstances whatever tolerate the slightest suspicion of cowardice or indiscipline, and I know from now on that none of you will present me with any such problem.

The speech was broken by meaningful pauses when Mountbatten's eyes ranged over the men lined up before him. It was as brilliant as the effect on his men was powerful. Few captains could have composed and memorised such an address in such a brief time, and certainly not with all the other responsibilities bearing down on him while under tow through waters that had already proved lethal.

The next morning, the dockyard mateys at Hawthorn, Leslie watched the return of the crippled *Kelly* in wonder. 'I thought we'd got rid of you for a bit.'

'Oh, but we like Hebburn, you know, the beer and the girls.'

There was not going to be much of either this time, as Mountbatten announced the following morning. It was only a few days to Christmas, and everyone was allowed home on leave. There was a great cheer at this, followed by dismay among some of the sailors who had no money for the rail ticket. Edwina had come up from London to join Mountbatten and to sympathise with him over his bad luck. When she heard of the dilemma, she said to her husband, 'I think I'd like to pay for everyone's leave fare.'

Mountbatten thought that an excellent idea. So did the *Kelly*'s company.

It took until early March 1940 before the *Kelly* was ready for sea again. Mountbatten, who had spent most of the time with other ships of his Flotilla – now complete – was thankful to be going north again. It was still bitter weather after one of the coldest winters on record, and they would be on North Sea convoy work, but he loathed inaction and was still awaiting the opportunity of making his mark with some spectacular success.

Mountbatten, as a signals specialist, and with his considerable experience of convoy work in dirty weather, was concerned about collisions when reactions to trouble had to be swift if lives were to be saved. The destroyer *Exmouth* had recently gone down with all hands without a signal; it had just disappeared without trace. To minimise the possibility of this occurring again, he arranged with 'Dusty' Dunsterville – his own and the Flotilla's Signals Officer – that there should be a standard and immediate signal made on hearing any sort of explosion. This was, 'Have been hit by mine or torpedo. Am uncertain which.'

On 9 March 1940, while escorting a North Sea convoy in company with several other destroyers in filthy weather, the *Kelly* ran into the stern of HMS *Gurkha*, which had just sunk a U-boat. Seconds later, with a long gash torn in the *Kelly*'s bows caused by the *Gurkha*'s propeller guard, the signal was made. The *Gurkha*, little damaged, answered the signal sardonically, 'That was not mine but me.' The story went round the Navy's flotillas with the speed of sound.

The accident was entirely the fault of the *Kelly*'s officer of the watch, who was not keeping an adequate lookout. Mountbatten was extraordinarily mild in his response and philosophical about having to return once more for repairs. Meanwhile, they lashed torpedo-mats over the thirty-foot-long tear and headed for the nearest port, Lerwick in the Shetlands. Here they reinforced their repairs, which Mountbatten insisted on testing by ordering twenty-six knots, to the anxiety of his officers who could not understand the need for such risk-taking.

At Scapa Flow, steel plates were welded over the gash, making it safe for Mountbatten to push up the speed as high as he liked, which was usually over thirty knots. 'We couldn't get into any of the northern yards,' Mounbatten recalled. 'It was infuriating. I particularly wanted the people at Hebburn to do the job, but they were too busy so we had to go down to the Thames, and the London graving dock.'

Very few of the men minded, though. Being a 'Chatham ship', many of them were Londoners, and they could surely look forward to some leave. It was mid-March when they docked, and leave for most of the crew was at once granted. Mountbatten and Edwina, who was working in London for the St John Ambulance, celebrated the arrival of the *Kelly* with a royal party. It was a very Mountbatten occasion, with the King and Queen heading the guest list, which included the Duke of Kent in RAF uniform with his beautiful wife Marina.

The *Kelly*'s damage was examined by all the guests as if it had been caused in some gallant action instead of through inefficiency, and after dinner Mountbatten put on a film show, always his favourite way of spending the evening. He had succeeded in acquiring an early print of Charlie Chaplin's *The Great Dictator*, which went down very well.

6

First Brush with Stukas

B ritain had been at war for seven months and almost the only fighting had been at sea, and for Mountbatten that had been interrupted by four mishaps which had kept the *Kelly* in dock for many weeks. Mountbatten had a number of simple axioms about war, most of them derived from his experiences at polo and his book, *Introduction to Polo*. 'Whenever you are doing nothing you are doing wrong,' was one. Another was that 'the same course of action cannot be advantageous to both sides, only to one. And if the opponent is not attacking it is because he does not wish to do so. If he is getting his way then that is disadvantageous to you.'

During the five weeks when the *Kelly* was being repaired again, Mountbatten spent most of his time at the Admiralty and among people who were running the war. 'Eden, Hore-Belisha and the rest all thought it was marvellous that there was no fighting. We were getting stronger every day, they said, and that was to our advantage, wasn't it?' Mountbatten recalled them claiming. 'I argued for all my worth, but they wouldn't budge. Only Churchill had the spirit of aggression running in his veins, he and one or two others like Leo Amery and of course the service chiefs. The Army in France was sitting on its backside and the RAF was fed up with dropping leaflets on the Germans. As for the French, they were terrified of upsetting the Germans and thought they were safe behind their Maginot Line. Time and again they refused permission for the RAF to drop mines into the River Rhine. It might lead to bombing of their cities, they said.'

Four years earlier, when Mountbatten was commanding the *Wishart* in the Mediterranean and war with Italy seemed imminent, he was instructed by the C-in-C to contact the French naval commander at Bizerta in a last-minute effort to form a joint policy. 'I knew him quite well', Mountbatten said, 'and I knew he spoke English. But when I arrived with the *Wishart*, do you know he wouldn't speak a word of English? And he ordered all his staff to talk French, too. . . . They were completely unco-operative and extremely rude to us.' Mountbatten was, however, able to discover that they had absolutely no war plans and only the vaguest idea of their harbour defences and so on.

Even Churchill had a certain confidence about the French Army and the political stability of the country derived from his experience in the First World War. Mountbatten had neither. 'I reckoned that between forty and fifty per cent of French servicemen were communist or unreliable or both.'

Besides 'Operation Catherine', Churchill had conceived plans for a pre-emptive strike on Norway, not to conquer that friendly country but to sever the vital German iron-ore route from Sweden. In winter, when the Baltic was frozen, the only supply route was by train for the short distance across Norway to Narvik, and thence down the 'Indreled' within Norwegian territorial waters, the same waters which the *City of Flint* used as an escape route. 'It must be understood', Churchill wrote, 'that an adequate supply of Swedish iron ore is vital to Germany and the interception or prevention of these Narvik supplies . . . will greatly reduce her power of resistance.'

The War Cabinet procrastinated and dissembled, just as they had over Churchill's Dardanelles plan twenty-six years earlier, when he would quote Euripides, 'The god of war hates those who hesitate.' By early April 1940, while the *Kelly* was still under repair, the green light was flashed. An Anglo-French force was ready to sail. But in the course of a last-minute delay, the Germans struck first. The British and French were completely outwitted, and in a sea-air blitzkrieg the capital of Norway and its chief ports were occupied almost overnight.

A counter-invasion was hastily conceived and an Anglo-French force, including a French Alpine Division, was despatched. The Norwegian campaign was under way. Except, briefly, at Narvik, the Allied forces never had a chance. Although the German Navy, responsible for bringing in the ground troops, was severely mauled and greatly outnumbered by Admiral Sir Charles Forbes's forces, the Germans gained and held on to almost total control of the air.

It was just as Mountbatten had predicted and feared. Oerlikons and larger calibre anti-aircraft guns could delay the destruction of a warship by bombers, but only fighter aircraft could protect them decisively. A great effort was made to get ashore a few obsolete Gladiator fighters, which for a time operated off a frozen lake, and a single squadron of Hurricanes, which also flew in off a carrier. But they were hopelessly outnumbered and soon had to be withdrawn, just as the troops, equally outnumbered, lacking artillery and anti-aircraft guns, had to be evacuated by the end of April.

This was the first of the evacuations which were to become a sombre feature of the early months of the war, and Mountbatten and the *Kelly* were to play their dangerous part in it.

Five days after the German landings in Norway, a major effort had been made to dislodge them from the important mid-Norwegian port of Trondheim. To support the frontal attack, two subsidiary landings were to be made, one of them to the north at the small town of Namsos. This assault was to be led by Major-General Adrian Carton de Wiart VC, the original of Evelyn Waugh's Colonel Ritchie-Hook in his novel *Men at Arms*. Carton de Wiart had been wounded nine times in the First World War, had lost an eye and gained a DSO – in addition to his VC – and a reputation for sublime bravery.

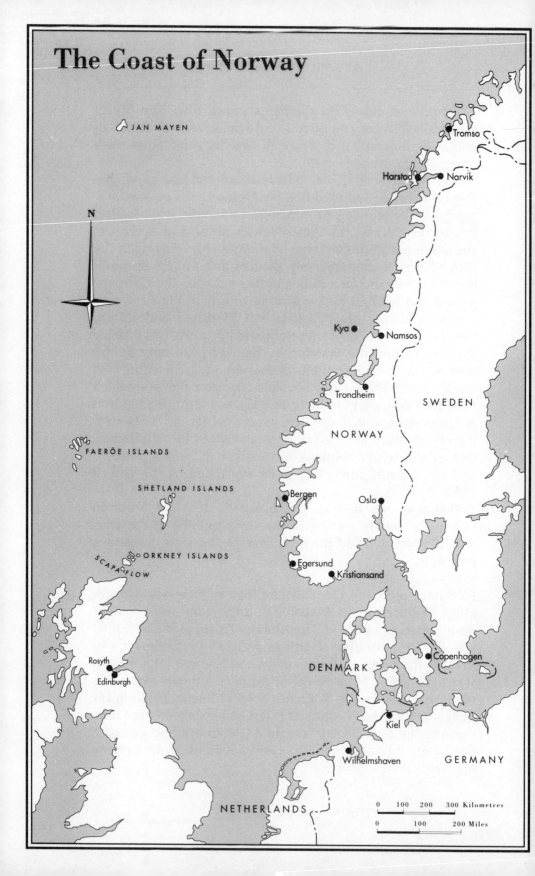

Carton de Wiart arrived at Namsos by flying-boat. Even before landing his party was under attack and a staff officer was wounded. 'Namsos was under four feet of snow,' Churchill recalled, 'and offered no concealment from the air. The enemy enjoyed complete air mastery, and we had neither anti-aircraft guns nor any airfield from which protecting squadrons might operate.' A few days after the landing from the sea, it is no surprise that he was reporting, 'The position of the Namsos force must be regarded as somewhat hazardous, but its commander is used to taking risks.'

Carton de Wiart's force, including a French Chasseur Alpin Brigade, was bombed and bombed again. A small group succeeded in advancing fifty miles, struggling through the snow and hostile terrain, but was forced back, and no amount of courage from the commander could possibly prevail against the hopeless odds. On 20 April a massive and unopposed bomber assault on the little port virtually flattened it. 'The whole place', wrote a naval eye-witness, 'was a mass of flames from end to end, and the glare on the snows of the surrounding mountains produced an unforgettable spectacle.'

On the following morning Carton de Wiart signalled, 'I see little chance of carrying out decisive, or indeed any, operations, unless enemy air activity is considerably restricted.' That was clearly impossible, and after more bombing and the advance on Namsos of strong German land forces, Carton de Wiart followed up with the message that there was no alternative but to evacuate. The Admiralty acted accordingly, though without air-cover Churchill knew that it would be a hazardous operation to extricate some 5,600 men from their self-made trap.

Since the start of the Norwegian campaign Mountbatten had been kicking his heels in London, with frequent visits to the dockyard to hasten repairs to the *Kelly*. He had heard with mixed feelings of the outcome of the first Battle of Narvik, when his old friend Captain Guy Warburton-Lee had led his own flotilla into Narvik and destroyed two enemy destroyers and sundry other ships. Warburton-Lee had commanded the *Witch* in the Mediterranean at the time when the *Wishart* had been made 'Cock of the Fleet', and they were great rivals as well as friends. To Mountbatten's distress, he also heard that while withdrawing, Warburton-Lee's destroyers had met five more heavy German destroyers; in the desperate duel that followed, Warburton-Lee had lost two of his ships and his own life. 'He also was awarded a posthumous VC,' Mountbatten recalled. 'What a great way to go!'

The second Battle of Narvik, fought three days later, intensified Mountbatten's impatience to get back into the shooting war. The battleship *Warspite* with nine destroyers had entered the fiord and extracted revenge for Warburton-Lee's death by sinking the remaining eight German destroyers and a U-boat.

The *Kelly* was ready for sea on 27 April and was immediately ordered north to Scapa Flow. Here Mountbatten learned that Vice-Admiral John Cunningham (no relation to Andrew) was to lead a rescue mission to Namsos, a town no one had heard of until recently. The troops there were more or less under siege from the ground and the air. At a commanders' conference Mountbatten learned that two British and one French cruiser and an anti-aircraft cruiser, with nine destroyers and three transports, were to carry out the operation on two nights, 1 and 2 May. Mountbatten himself was to lead a division of four destroyers, which would go in first to clear the way for the escorted transports.

Cunningham's strong force cleared Scapa Flow and made best speed north-east across the North Sea. Early in the morning they were spotted by German aircraft and experienced their first bombing while still far from their destination. It was high-level bombing and, just as he had feared, restriction to forty-degrees elevation of his 4.7-inch guns proved frustrating. None of the ships was hit, but for most of the men it was their first experience of being bombed, and an omen of what was to come.

They approached the Norwegian coast. Fog closed about them, and they were forced to heave to at Kya Light near the entrance to Nansen fiord. Messages flashed between the ships. There was no question of the larger ships entering pilotage waters, but Mountbatten thought that it was essential to make contact with Carton de Wiart and attempt to evacuate some of the troops from the town. He therefore volunteered to take in his division in spite of the risks.

'The moment permission was granted, I began a mad dash along the seventy or so miles. It was 5 a.m. Suddenly the fog cleared, like a curtain pulled aside,' Mountbatten remembered. 'A hundred yards ahead was a mass of half-submerged rocks. So it was full astern, and we missed them by yards.'

'Mad dash' was the correct definition of this advance on the beleaguered town. There was no need for this twenty-six-knot frenzy, putting at risk five destroyers which had an important function to fulfil.

So now it was 'hide-and-seek with the German bombers, in and out of scattered fog banks'. And still they were bombed, one of his destroyers being hit, killing or injuring twenty-three men. Mountbatten was puzzled and alarmed, and it was not until later that he realised that, like so many ostriches with their heads in the sand, the tips of their masts stuck out of the fog into the sunlight above.

Namsos itself appeared suddenly in a fog clearance, the town – or what was left of it – still burning from the most recent raid. 'It was a dreadful sight, nothing but smashed buildings, jetties and storehouses, smoke rising above.'

The bombers came back before they could close the harbour with its groups of waiting troops. There was no alternative but to steer back into the fog and withdraw. Mountbatten accepted temporary defeat and led his ships back to Kya Light, using Asdic most of the way.

Cunningham had now decided on a night evacuation, whatever the conditions, and divided his force in two. The *Kelly* went off on her own in the sub-Arctic dusk. There was no fog and, for the present, no bombers. 'We went up the fiord at twenty-six knots, between the snow-capped peaks and the lush valleys with their wooden farmhouses. It was all incredibly peaceful, and I remember saying to myself, "This

can't be war. . . ." But it was.' That was how Mountbatten
described this second attempt.

It was 10.15 p.m. when Namsos came into sight again, the
smoke still rising into the twilight northern sky. 'We were
signalling, "Come on up – come on up!" to the rest of the
Flotilla,' Dunsterville recalled. 'Namsos was a terrible sight
and yet strangely quiet. There were a lot of dying fires and a
trawler was still burning. We got alongside a damaged jetty
and at once over two hundred chasseurs came on-board with
their great packs, and their heavy boots making a terrible row
on our steel decks.'

'They were ferocious-looking men with heavy packs, made
heavier by the great cheeses they had looted,' one of the
Kelly's ratings recalled. 'Gave them a hand off with their
gear', said another laconically, 'and at the same time spirited
a few cheeses away into the larder.'

Briefly ashore, Mountbatten made contact with 'old Carton de Wiart, one eye gleaming defiance'. Later, when the
transports and other ships followed the Kelly and took off
everyone else, the General commented, 'It was a tremendous
undertaking to embark that whole force in a night of three
short hours, but the Navy did it and earned my undying
gratitude.'

Not a man had been left behind, but as in most evacuations by sea, the shore was littered with vehicles and
stacks of arms and ammunition. The destroyer Afridi lingered
briefly to shell them, starting yet another blaze and causing
many explosions before racing off after the other ships.
These had formed up into line ahead in the half-light of
a fog-free dawn, the anti-aircraft cruiser Carlisle taking up
the rear.

The first enemy plane was sighted at 4.30 a.m. and
disappeared again with her report. 'Luckily by this time',
Dunsterville remembered, 'we had got out as fast as we
could and it really was a case of sauve qui peut.'

Half an hour later the transports and their escort saw the
first dive-bombing Stukas come in, like avenging birds of
prey. Everyone had heard about Stukas. They had featured
in numerous magazine and newspaper reports on the Polish

campaign, when they had wiped out airfields, communications and towns alike. Accompanying photographs showed the menacing configuration of the Ju 87, with her heavily canted wings, spatted fixed undercarriage and long cockpit canopy housing pilot and rear gunner. Wing slats which could be extended to ninety degrees slowed down the plane in a seventy–eighty degree dive, while sirens mounted in each undercarriage leg added psychological terror to the attack. At this time she normally carried a single 500 kg. or two 250 kg. bombs. A hit on a destroyer by the first would certainly sink her, while many were sunk by a single 250 kg. bomb. The Stuka, operating at any height between 8,000 and 15,000 feet, on sighting her target, turned over on to her back and went into her steep dive. Targets might be selected between pilots of the *Stukagruppe* on the way down. The bombs were carried on a cradle hinged aft of the radiator bath, which was swung forward during the dive so that they cleared the airscrew on release, which might be as low as 400 feet. Her great merit as a tactical weapon was her accuracy, but the Stuka was vulnerable to light anti-aircraft fire and modern fighters.

'I had given a lot of thought to destroyer defence against air attack because I knew how vulnerable we could be, not so much from high-level bombing but from dive-bombing,' Mountbatten told this writer. 'By watching carefully, it was not difficult to evade the bombs dropped from a height with our outstanding manoeuvrability, and our acceleration and deceleration. The great thing was to keep up a high speed and jink about, just as bombers attempted to evade heavy anti-aircraft fire by doing the unexpected.

'The same principle was applied in dive-bombing attacks: speed, evasion and holding the light anti-aircraft fire until the Stuka was at the bottom of her dive. I also calculated that by going full astern at the last minute, you could tempt the pilot into too steep a dive and even beyond ninety degrees – and that meant curtains for him. We had at least one success using this method.' This last claim was, alas, a figment of Mountbatten's imagination. Such a manoeuvre was beyond the powers of the most skilfully handled destroyer.

The Stukas selected for this attack were from *Stukagruppe* I/StG1, commanded by Major Walter Hagen, which had originally operated from Stavanger but had recently moved north to Trondheim. The sky was clear, the light adequate, and these pilots had never had such a tempting target at sea. But the anti-aircraft fire from the *Carlisle* in particular, and the other cruisers, was unexpectedly heavy and accurate. The sky was spotted with the dark puffs of exploding 4-inch and 4.7-inch shells, and when they were in their dive the pom-pom fire, and then the .5-inch and .303-inch light fire, seemed to fill the air.

The bombs exploding in the water sent up tall spouts of white water, and several near hits drenched the gun crews and bridge personnel amid the scream of sirens. It was not until the third wave that the Stukas had their first success. The French destroyer *Bison*, crammed with rescued troops, was hit and set on fire, a disaster distantly witnessed by the *Kelly*. As she came to a halt and began to settle, carley rafts and one or two boats were launched and many of the panic-stricken soldiers hurled themselves into the icy water. It was not only the cold that put them at risk. The Stukas, hovering about their victim like jackals, came down low and machine-gunned the men as they attempted to escape from the destroyer's inferno.

Captain Philip Vian raced the *Afridi* towards the *Bison* and began picking up survivors while attempting to hold off the bombers. For half an hour it was a scene of chaos and confusion, the *Afridi*'s crew doing all they could to drag the unfortunate men from their boats and the water.

At last she steamed off, intent on catching up with the rest of the force. She never made it. The next Stuka attack by a single plane led to two hits by 250 kg. bombs. The *Afridi* came to a halt in a cloud of mixed steam and smoke, and within a few minutes quietly capsized. It was a miracle that only 100 lives were lost, the rest being picked up by two destroyers which raced to her rescue.

The Norwegian coast was a smudge on the eastern horizon when the last of the bomber attacks took place in the mid-afternoon. Several Stukas, almost beyond their range, spotted the distant *Kelly* far out to sea and were provoked into an attempt to sink her. Leading Seaman Sidney Mosses of the ship's pom-pom crew steadied himself for the inevitable attack, while Mountbatten evaded with the *Kelly* on full helm port and starboard and back to port again, all the anti-aircraft crews attempting to keep on their target with the ever-changing angle of aim and deflection. But it was Mosses's men who 'got their man', nobody argued over that. The 'Chicago piano' had the greatest range and they caught the Stuka several thousand feet before she was due to drop her bombs. With flames and smoke trailing behind her, the bomber just kept straight on down, an awful and awe-inspiring sight as she plunged into the sea 1,000 yards away from her intended victim. There was never a chance of the crew getting out and they were probably dead when they hit the sea.

By dusk on 4 May the transports and accompanying warships were out of range of the Stukas, too, and in two groups made an untroubled crossing of the North Sea to Scapa Flow. Under Vice-Admiral John Cunningham, the evacuation operation had been a resounding success. The only army casualties were those who had gone down with the *Bison* and the *Afridi*, no more than a hundred troops in all out of 5,600 who would inevitably have become casualties or made prisoners of war.

'Twilight War', Churchill has written, 'ended with Hitler's assault on Norway.' The Allied Norwegian campaign to attempt to drive the German forces out of that country featured many acts of courage by all three services. The Fleet Air Arm with its obsolete aircraft had sunk an enemy cruiser by dive-bombing, its first success in the war. Captain Warburton-Lee's action at Narvik was in the highest traditions of naval initiative, skill and courage. RAF fighter pilots, who had never before been on-board an aircraft carrier, took off and flew to strange landing-grounds in mountainous terrain. Even more spectacular was the successful landing on a carrier at sea of an entire squadron of Hurricane fighters, lacking arrester hooks, without mishap at the close of the campaign, only to be lost when the *Gneisenau* and *Scharnhorst* sank the carrier soon after. Soldiers, ill-equipped for fighting in thick snow at low temperatures, fought manfully without supporting artillery or anti-aircraft guns.

But it had been a miserable business of poor planning, vacillation, misunderstanding and bungling, which pointed depressingly to the failure of the Allied High Command to absorb any of the lessons of the First World War, predominantly the Dardanelles campaign of 1915. The only strikingly successful aspect of it all, as at the Dardanelles, was the evacuation, thanks largely to the Navy. It was just as well for there were plenty more to come.

It was some satisfaction to Mountbatten and the *Kelly's* men that they had survived the hazards of Namsos without a mishap and had actually recorded a minor victory to offset all their past troubles. Mountbatten recorded:

As we steamed back across the North Sea, out of range at last of the German bombers, I thought about my father, who never saw any action in all his years in the Royal Navy. I hated war as much as he did, but he would have envied me that action off Namsos, just as he had loved to listen to [his brother] Georgie's descriptions of the naval actions he fought in the North Sea.

The German Navy had been heavily disabled in the Norwegian campaign. It was a price Hitler was prepared to pay. Like Napoleon, he never fully understood the meaning of sea-power and took an ambivalent attitude towards his Navy and his admirals. Only the U-boat force enjoyed his unbroken support from the first day of war, and the U-boat commanders were regarded as the greatest of all his heroes.

Among the German ships sunk was the new and formidable heavy-cruiser *Blücher*, which was, surprisingly, sent to the bottom along with senior administrative staff and senior members of the Gestapo intended to take over control of the Norwegian capital. She was the victim of land-based torpedoes and shore batteries outside Oslo, and marked one of the few Norwegian successes. Two light-cruisers were also lost in the campaign, and in the battles at Narvik almost the entire German destroyer force had been lost. Eight U-boats had also gone down.

In the short term the heavily damaged ships were even more weakening, including as they did both of Germany's battle-cruisers, *Scharnhorst* and *Gneisenau*, the pocket battle-ship *Lützow*, the heavy-cruiser *Hipper* and a light-cruiser.

Although the German surface ships were to give plenty of trouble later in the war, especially the giant *Bismarck* and *Tirpitz*, the damage suffered off Norway in April to June 1940 had an important effect on the course of the war at sea.

There were, however, light German coastal forces still present in the North Sea at the time when the *Kelly* returned from Namsos, and one of them was to play an important role in the eventful log of Mountbatten's ship.

7

'Damn the torpedoes'

ADMIRAL DAVID FARRAGUT, MOBILE BAY, 1864

The return of the evacuation forces from Namsos marked the failure of the campaign to drive the conquering Germans out of Norway, and the threat of more formidable action far to the south where the Allied forces on the Maginot Line had faced the German forces on the Siegfried Line for eight uneventful months. All intelligence reports now suggested that at last the Panzers were about to move, and that 'the blitz in the west' was on.

Almost as important to the Germans as the iron-ore coastal traffic off the Norwegian coast was the coastal shipping plying between Hamburg and Bremen and the neutral ports of Rotterdam, Amsterdam and Antwerp. Little had been done by the Allies to interfere with this trade, in part because of the self-imposed restrictions on the RAF from bombing enemy merchantmen. These originated in the 1923 'Draft Hague Rules of Air Warfare', which had not been ratified by any nation, were not incorporated in international law and were not adhered to by Germany, which had been attacking British coastal traffic since the outbreak of war by aircraft, mines and E-boats.

In March, and again in April during the Norwegian campaign, these rules were relaxed, and Mountbatten and the *Kelly*, with the 5th Flotilla, were drawn south from one dying fire of war to the threatened conflagration which would soon consume Holland and Belgium, and then France itself. They were at Londonderry, with the *Kandahar* (Commander Geoffrey Robson), when Mountbatten got his orders to rendezvous with the cruiser *Birmingham*, flying the flag of Admiral Charles Layton, and other destroyers in the southern North Sea. It was a long passage, right round the north of Scotland. Admiralty intelligence was at this time receiving an increasing number of reports of enemy movements at sea, matching the rising tide of information on German troop movements and the alerting of Luftwaffe forces along Germany's western frontiers. One of these naval reports concerned a German mine-laying group, supported by E-boats, operating off the island of Sylt, just off the frontier between Germany and German-occupied Denmark.

The *Kelly* and the *Kandahar* picked up the destroyer *Bulldog*, a fine thirty-five-knot boat, a predecessor to Mountbatten's *Daring*, and headed out for Sylt on the morning of 9 May.

'It was around 6 p.m. when an aircraft reported that it had spotted a U-boat and forced it to dive,' Mountbatten recounted. 'I ordered *Kandahar* to join me in a hunt. We soon began to hear pings, and "Egg" Burnett thought we were close enough for a depth-charge attack, which we duly carried out.'

The Captain of the *Kandahar* took a different view and recalled that he was reluctant to leave the main force on what he believed would turn out to be a waste of time and contrary to their instructions. But he knew of Mountbatten's longing to score a confirmed U-boat victory, which was automatically rewarded with a DSO.

The *Birmingham* was still over the eastern horizon somewhere, awaiting her escort anxiously while the two destroyers dashed to and fro in search of the supposed U-boat. After another fifteen minutes Robson could no longer resist signalling, 'I think it is time we were going.' Mountbatten evidently did not agree and signalled back, 'Give it another twenty minutes.'

At the end of this time dusk was closing in and with every passing minute their chance of joining the *Birmingham* became more remote. A further anxiety was the state of their fuel reserves. Eight hours earlier, at noon, Commander Mike Evans had reported the fuel state at forty-five per cent; since then they had been steaming at high speed for hundreds of miles, when consumption rose greatly. Evans was checking again now and working out how much fuel they would need to get back to port at economical cruising speed, based on the *Kelly*'s total capacity of oil at 484 tons and consumption at 2.3 nautical miles per ton.

Evans reported his findings to Mountbatten on the bridge, and it was decided that they should maintain their present course until 11 p.m., when they would have to return if meanwhile they had not rejoined the *Birmingham*. One officer recalled, 'The whole operation was already assuming the ominous shape of a botch, and, like Commander Robson, I was becoming increasingly concerned about the *Birmingham* being on her own in distinctly hostile waters.' The men were told that they could fall out from action stations but to be ready for instant recall if required.

It was a slightly misty late evening, no stars or moon being visible. It was pleasantly warm in the boiler-room as always, but on deck it was noticeably chilly. One of the stokers, off duty from the boiler-room, put on extra clothes to sit on deck with the gun crew of one of the twin 4.7s. He was still evidently cold and one of the crew invited him, 'Hey, Stokes, come and park your arse on this valve'; he did so thankfully. Others went down the ladders in search of a mug of hot cocoa. Mountbatten was on his second mug. It was a drink he loved all his life.

From the bridge of the *Kandahar*, like the *Kelly* steaming without lights, a signal lamp was seen flashing like a search-light in the intense darkness. Robson was appalled. 'This is ridiculous!' he exclaimed to David Milford Haven, who was puzzled when he read it: 'How are the muskets? Let battle commence.' What on earth was his uncle up to? If it was some quotation, it meant nothing to him.

These waters were known to be infested with E-boats. This light-flashing might as well have been a signal to a nearby E-boat to launch her torpedoes, for almost at once the two officers on the *Kandahar*'s bridge saw a great sheet of flame envelop the *Kelly*, followed instantly by a rising cloud of smoke and steam illuminated by the flames.

'Oh Christ!' Robson exclaimed. 'She's gone.' A few seconds later he ordered full speed out of the area.

'Can't we stay and search for survivors, sir?' Milford Haven asked in anguish.

'Certainly not.'

Captain Guy Warburton-Lee, killed a month earlier in Narvik fiord and one of the most highly regarded destroyer captains, had always advocated keeping clear of a torpedoed destroyer for fear of further destruction. It was a lesson which should have been learned as long before as 1914, when, in turn, three big cruisers had been sunk while seeking to rescue survivors with terrible extra loss of life.

When at length Robson considered it safe to return, he found the *Kelly* still afloat and under tow by the *Bulldog*. 'Is Captain (D) alive?' he signalled; back came the answer promptly, 'Yes, you are not in command of the Flotilla yet!'

A few minutes later, Mountbatten followed up this satisfying signal by ordering the *Kandahar* to come alongside at first light and take off the injured. Meanwhile, *Bulldog*, making scarcely five knots with her burden, had signalled the Admiralty, '*Kelly* has been torpedoed 56.48 N. 05.09 E.,' and the *Birmingham* and Scapa Flow, 'Assistance required immediately,' followed by the position. With luck, a towing tug or two would be with them within thirty-six hours. Meanwhile, they just had to abide by the *Kelly*'s motto and 'Keep On'.

One of the most demanding aspects of their plight was to steer the *Kelly* without power or communications. There were a dozen ratings down in the tiller flat steering the ship by hand, and the only way to get orders to them was through a chain of men from the bridge to the hatch leading down to the tiller flat. All night long the orders 'Port thirty-five', 'Starboard thirty-five' or 'Amidships' were transmitted by human voice, with the men from time to time changing jobs to reduce boredom and keep awake.

When the E-boat made her extraordinary appearance in the night, crashing along the *Kelly*'s side, her 20 mm. gun was firing, the trigger jammed or perhaps with a dead German seaman's hand locked upon it. 'I remember ducking behind the bridge screen', Mountbatten recalled, 'and thinking to myself, "What a damn silly thing to do!" So I straightened up and watched the rest of the action. Later someone recovered the E-boat's steering-wheel and gave it to me. I've kept it ever since.'

Several times during that long night Mountbatten ordered an extra rum issue, and the rum helped to keep the men going. Twice the cable parted and had to be renewed in the darkness, using minimum light. With the first touch of dawn Mountbatten could see that the *Kelly*'s list had increased and that with the rising sea she was taking in more water. At the same time the *Birmingham* hove into sight. 'Thank Christ she's all right!' Dunsterville remembers thinking. 'Leaving the cruiser alone was about the worst gaffe Mountbatten ever committed.'

Admiral Layton was clearly astonished at the sight of the *Kelly* and did not believe that Mountbatten could get her home. 'Suggest that you abandon ship and scuttle her,' he signalled. 'Risks involved too great for salvage value.'

Mountbatten would have none of it and always claimed that his answer was, 'I do not require your services any more, thank you. I will get home by myself if you can spare me a tug.' We can be sure that he was more circumspect in his language than this, but it was inappropriate for the Admiral to order a captain to scuttle his ship, so he left Mountbatten, signalling encouragement for his efforts.

The miserable task of burying the dead was undertaken as the cruiser disappeared to the west. Mountbatten conducted a brief service as corpse after corpse, or what was left of a corpse, dug from the wreckage below, was lowered into the sea in canvas shrouds. Then, with great difficulty in the rising seas, Robson brought the *Kandahar* alongside, and the wounded were slung across to her. Soon after this operation had been completed, bombers were sighted.

On this day of all days, with the Panzers crossing the

German frontiers from before dawn and the Luftwaffe fully involved in smashing airfields, roads, railways and forts as well as cities like Rotterdam, it might be thought that the bombers would not have bothered with a half-sunk destroyer. But several Dornier Do 17s came down low, dropping bombs and machine-gunning the decks of the *Bulldog*, *Kandahar* and *Kelly*. They were met with fierce anti-aircraft fire. 'I worked a .5-inch multiple machine-gun,' Mountbatten reported, 'and I must say that it's much more satisfactory actually firing a gun than just sitting there when you are being attacked!'

As the day wore on the plight of the *Kelly* steadily worsened. Mountbatten reckoned that she might capsize at any time, and they had ditched all the top weight already. 'The sea got up and the ship started to develop a very unpleasant slow roll. I could feel that we were very near to a complete loss of stability. I racked my brains to think of more top weight that I could get rid of. And then I had a brainwave,' Mountbatten said later. '"The ship's company," I exclaimed. "They weigh a hell of a lot [some ten tons actually]. Let's get rid of the ship's company." So the whole ship's company was transferred to the escorting destroyers.' This was carried out in the midst of another bombing attack, though this time the anti-aircraft guns actually drove the Dorniers away.

Later, Mountbatten wrote, 'On returning to harbour the designer of the *Kelly*, A. P. Cole, carried out certain calculations which showed that if I had not removed the surviving ship's company the ship would undoubtedly have gone over before we got her back.'

At dawn after their second night, two tugs were sighted and came alongside. 'Where shall we take you?' asked the senior officer. 'To the Tyne,' Mountbatten answered at once. So it was back to Hawthorn, Leslie once again. And by happy chance the one member of the *Kelly*'s company who had remained on-board, the ship's cat Hawthorn, was discovered to have given birth to kittens in an open drawer of the Navigator's desk during the night. She was found by one of the twelve volunteer ratings who returned on-board with Mountbatten and five officers to manage the ship under tow.

All that day, the following night and day – for ninety-one hours in all – the *Kelly* wallowed through seas that threatened to consume her. The tug tow parted again. One report ran:

> They spent half the night getting rid of the broken tow-wire and getting a new one fitted. All the work had to be done by hand. Captain, officers and men heaved and strained on the greasy, lively wire until it was in place and once more they were under way and heading for home.

The word had got around Tyneside that the *Kelly* was on her way home again. When a crowd sighted the half-submerged wreck coming up the river, they let out a spontaneous cheer. Then, in turn, the shipyard men left their work and shouted their welcome. Every ship of every size that had the steam sounded their sirens. Some of the *Kelly*'s men, filthy, unshaven and tired almost beyond endurance, succumbed to tears at this welcome and their own salvation. Their ship was secured alongside a cruiser, and they walked across her decks to dry land again.

It was now 13 May, and Mountbatten wrote in his diary:

> After many vicissitudes we reached the Tyne in the evening and were towed to the accompaniment of cheers all up the river. After dining on-board the *Kandahar*, I went as I was, no luggage, unshaven and filthy, to the Station Hotel and after ninety-one hours in tow a real bed was heaven.

In terms of logic and cost, Admiral Layton had been right to recommend abandoning and scuttling the *Kelly*. So severe was her damage that it would have been cheaper and easier to lay down a new keel and start all over again. Then again, the *Kelly*, properly handled, should never have been in a position to be torpedoed. The wild-goose chase after a probably non-existent U-boat when she and the *Kandahar* should have rendezvoused with the *Birmingham* was highly irresponsible. But misjudgments notwithstanding, war is not made up of mathematical accounts, of simple debits and credits. When the story of those days and nights of struggle against hopeless odds and final triumphant survival was told, it raised the spirits of the entire nation. And with the conquest of France and the Low Countries and the threat of invasion closer than at any time since Napoleon, that benefit might be incalculable but was considerable.

It was a pity, therefore, that the courageous and triumphant episode of the *Kelly* had a somewhat unseemly aftermath. Having failed to convince the Admiralty that the *Kelly* had sunk a single U-boat, let alone two, Mountbatten was confident that his saving his ship from her seemingly inevitable fate would surely bring him his DSO. Instead, he was outraged to discover that he had been merely 'mentioned in despatches'. Churchill, always an admirer of gallantry and now Premier, considered this a bit mean, too, and minuted that Mountbatten should surely be due for the DSO. Mountbatten's cousin, the Duke of Kent, also agreed to put in a good word for him in high places. It did not work. 'If the King's brother cannot get his cousin the same decoration as every other captain (D) has been given, then the powers working against me must be very strong indeed,' Mountbatten commented sharply, but inaccurately.

Mountbatten was certain that the most important power working against him was Admiral Sir Charles Forbes, C-in-C Home Fleet. Forbes had been Admiral Commanding the Mediterranean destroyers before the war at a time when no one could fail to observe, and sometimes to disapprove of, Mountbatten's flamboyant life style. Lord Beaverbrook, the Canadian-born newspaper millionaire who was better informed than any of his rivals, cautioned Mountbatten through an intermediary, 'Tell Dickie that Winston warned me that Forbes means to break him.'

For once, Beaverbrook had got it all wrong. Forbes was much too big a man to let his judgment be prejudiced by his personal feelings. What he did make clear, however, was that, due to various mishaps, the *Kelly* had been at sea during the war for exactly fifty-seven days in over eight months, and that the crippling of the ship once again was caused by Mountbatten's own misjudgment and carelessness, not to say disregard of orders.

Mountbatten remained outraged at this slight, which reflected on his officers and men, too, and used every means to recover his damaged reputation. His wife Edwina, who knew almost everyone in high places, did her best, but he begged her to make clear that she was not working directly on his behalf. 'If you like to learn up the arguments by heart and make out you got them from any of my officers direct – I cannot see there is any harm in that.'

But the only satisfaction Mountbatten derived from all this was that Admiral Forbes was superseded by Admiral Jack Tovey later in the year. Ever since Churchill had been appointed First Lord of the Admiralty in 1911 he had been having rows with admirals, nearly all of whom he thought inadequate in one way or another. And Forbes's treatment of Mountbatten was only one of numerous incidents that had contributed to Churchill's judgment that the Admiral was an old fuddy-duddy lacking an aggressive and positive spirit. The official judgment on him was different: 'His steady hand on the reins controlling our vital maritime power contributed greatly to bringing the country through this anxious period with its maritime strength not only unimpaired but growing.' Mountbatten never forgave Forbes, and he told George VI that Forbes disliked him 'for talking too much and not being sufficiently humble'.

It would be many months before the *Kelly* was ready for sea again. Previous mishaps had led to the replacement of the bow and stern sections. Now it was not only a matter of a new midships section. A new boiler-room and flanking bulkheads were needed and all the relating compartments and the bridge. 'The new midships section', ran one report, 'hung above the drydock bottom in a rigor mortis of torn and frantically twisted metal.' In the end, the whole ship was stripped down to her bare structure, so that she looked as she had on the stocks in the spring of 1938.

When Cole came to look at her soon after her return, he could feel justifiably proud of the survival capacity of his design thanks to the longitudinal form of hull construction. But to the regret of Mountbatten, his officers and men, the *Kelly* had to be decommissioned and the company dispersed, though many of them made it known that they wished to return when the time came for her to be commissioned again.

'This was very gratifying,' Mountbatten admitted, adding with amazingly untypical modesty, 'After all they have been through I was surprised that any of them wanted to serve under me again. Meanwhile I shifted my staff down to Immingham [Hull, on the River Humber] with the rest of the Flotilla on anti-invasion duties.' Nine destroyers had been sunk during the Dunkirk evacuation and no fewer than twenty-three damaged. Without them, the troops (or most of them) would never have got off at all, but it was a high price to pay. As in the First World War, and in Nelson's time with frigates, there were never enough of them.

The fall of France meant not only the loss of the support of almost all her Navy, but with the conquest of Norway, Denmark, Holland and Belgium as well, the Royal Navy now faced an unbroken hostile coastline from north Norway to Bordeaux, along with all these nations' naval bases and airfields. It also meant that the U-boats, based now on France's west-coast ports instead of having to travel north round Scotland before reaching their operational area, could more than double the length of their patrols.

With the entry of Italy into the war, when her ally had conquered most of the rest of Europe, the Royal Navy's responsibilities were greatly extended. The whole of the Mediterranean had also become a hostile sea, from Gibraltar to Malta and on to Alexandria. When the *Kelly* was due to recommission, months ahead of schedule, the naval scene was to be even more dangerous than at the time when she had been blown up.

Meanwhile, Mountbatten booked in at the County Hotel at Immingham on the Humber and administered his Flotilla from there; from time to time he went to sea with the mixed 'J' and 'K' ships which formed 'The Fighting Fifth'. In this way, he could note the style and quality of his captains and their officers.

It is never comfortable to have one's Captain (D) and his staff imposed on one [wrote Anthony Pugsley, Captain of the *Javelin*]. Apart from the dislocation and discomfort of having to provide accommodation, which includes the Captain of the ship having to vacate his cabin, there is the embarrassment of two senior officers functioning from the same small space on the bridge. The Captain (D) is in command of the Flotilla as a whole but not, under these circumstances, of the ship in which he is embarked . . . a considerable amount of tact was required from all concerned if friction was not to occur and, fortunately, with this Mountbatten was well equipped.

Pugsley also noted how welcome Mountbatten's visits to the ward-room of the *Javelin* were. 'My officers would crowd round him to enjoy his conversation with far less diffidence than they would show with other senior officers.'

The work at this time was mainly sweeps and patrols and covering minelayers and minesweepers, both highly vulnerable vessels, in coastal waters. On one night with Mountbatten in command of the *Jupiter* and in company with the *Javelin*, the two destroyers were escorting the minelayers *Esk* and *Ivanhoe*. Both, hoist with their own petard, ran on to a German minefield off the Friesian Islands. One minelayer had her back broken, the other her bows blown off back to the bridge.

The officer-of-the-watch of the *Jupiter*, Lieutenant John Jones, recalled, 'Lord Louis had to make a decision either (a) to go on to the minefield and get them off and risk losing *Jupiter* and *Javelin*, or (b) leave them there. If (a) failed and the destroyers had been lost, he would have been blamed for recklessness. If he decided on (b), he would have faced criticism of an unpleasant nature.'

This time luck was with Mountbatten. The *Jupiter* towed out the *Esk* with no more trouble and got her back to the Humber and the *Javelin* succeeded in pulling out the *Ivanhoe* from this dangerous area. But still there was no DSO.

In September the 5th Flotilla was moved down to Plymouth to operate in the Western Approaches. 'Things were a great deal more interesting working out of Plymouth,' Mountbatten recounted. 'Almost as soon as we arrived we were sent off with the old fifteen-inch gun battleship *Revenge*, which had fought at Jutland, to bombard Cherbourg.' Their main target was four of Germany's few remaining big destroyers, each loaded with some sixty mines. 'It was an entertaining exercise. My destroyer got in close in the dark and we each put in a hundred rounds of 4.7-inch shells in just over three minutes. Then our battleship opened up and that was a great sight.'

In the midst of all this uproar Bomber Command came over the port and added to the mayhem. The German defences were already blazing away into the night sky believing that the sea bombardment was bombing from the air, and it was not until the *Revenge* and her escort withdrew that the eleven-inch coastal defence guns opened up. 'Then we saw a rippling flash astern of us as the shore battery opened up and, a few seconds later, there was the roar of passing heavy shells,' recalled the *Javelin*'s Captain. 'As they hit the sea, tall columns of water slowly rose, ghost-like, between us and the *Revenge* and as slowly subsided.'

'Great fun and a great sight,' noted Mountbatten, who was unaware that neither the shelling nor the bombing had found any of the destroyers, which were moored some distance from the main dock area, and later left for Brest which they thought would be safer.

It became known soon after the withdrawal of the *Revenge* and her destroyers that the German destroyers, with their excellent radar, located a British minelaying force and sank one of the ships. Mountbatten was thoroughly rattled by these exploits and determined to pin down and teach the Germans a lesson. Every night he led four of his Flotilla out on a sweep, and on the night of 24–25 November it was the *Javelin's* turn again to accommodate him.

Captain Dunsterville today recalls how everyone hated this unpredictable changing from one ship to the other: 'I didn't have my own signals ratings. Mountbatten also insisted on steaming in oblique line ahead, the idea being that you gained half a knot by avoiding the wake of the ship ahead. But that meant you could turn sharply in only one direction according to whether you were oblique to port or starboard. But speed was everything. In fact on search operations like these it was a great disadvantage. You can't see anything for spray over the bridge, and the noise you make from the fans and engines can be heard for miles around.'

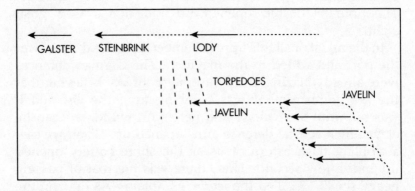

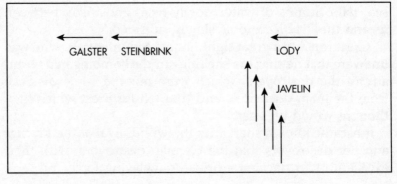

The German destroyers were out again that night and, so Hans Bartel, Commander of the *Karl Galster*, claimed, they saw the British destroyers on their radar, confirmed by the terrific noise, for around four minutes before they spotted them visually.

Mountbatten did not spot the three German ships until 2,000 yards range. 'Closed to 1,000 yards. . . . Our shots went over the Germans and theirs over me.'

'Put your sights down, you fools,' someone on the *Javelin*'s bridge shouted facetiously. 'You'll never hit us.' It was not a wise or accurate prediction.

Commander Pugsley said to Mountbatten, 'Straight on at 'em, I presume, sir?'

To his dismay, Mountbatten replied, 'No, no, we must turn on a parallel course at once or they will get away from us.' And, turning to the Signals Officer, he ordered, 'Flotilla turn ninety degrees to port together.'

Pugsley wrote later,

Our turn to port was disastrous. Not only did it throw the gun-director off his dimly-seen target as the ship, careening wildly over, swung round at high speed, but it offered to the enemy a perfect target for his torpedoes.

To compound their troubles, the Germans had the advantage of using flashless cordite while the British guns had only full flash, further obscuring the enemy and half-blinding everyone.

'At that moment two torpedoes hit us,' Mountbatten reported laconically later, 'one in the bows and the other in the stern, and then our after magazine blew up. Maddening to be put out of action but lucky to escape with fifty killed and bow and stern blown off.'

In fact three officers, including the doctor, and forty-three ratings were killed in this double disaster. 'I think it must have been then that I got a splinter near my left eye,' Dunsterville remembered, 'but I didn't know it until Mountbatten said, "What's the matter with you, Flags?", and I found I was bleeding. I washed it off and thought no more about it.'

Pugsley recorded:

> The world went up in flame and destruction around me. A torpedo struck home under the forecastle. Almost simultaneously another hit near the stern, its explosion being followed by a third and even more tremendous one as the after magazine blew up. . . . On the bridge I found myself lying amidst a heap of humanity in a corner. As the gallant ship recovered from the blow and heaved herself more or less upright again, I was amazed to find most of us unharmed, including Lord Louis – though he afterwards complained that I trod on his face as I struggled to my feet.

Pugsley then made a quick inspection of the damage, caused he believed entirely by Mountbatten's misjudgment. He reported:

> Forward, the forecastle and the forward gun turret had vanished; but below there was even more serious damage as all compartments forward of the boiler-rooms were flooded. Aft, following the magazine explosion, the oil fuel tanks caught fire and blazed furiously, defeating for a long while all efforts to subdue the flames. Below the surface the twisted, shattered remains of the after end of the ship hung down until, some half an hour after the explosion, this mass of metal suddenly sheared off and sank.

'We were left in the middle bit of *Javelin*,' remarked Alistair 'Guns' Robin. 'One of my memories is that breakfast was still sizzling on the hob. All we could do was to sit down and have bacon and eggs and await somebody to come and pick up the bits.'

It was a great credit to the design that the *Javelin* continued to float. The starboard bow had been forced back square to the deck, and the port side was in fragments. The second

4.7-inch gun turrets were pointing up at an angle that theoretically could have shot at any plane. The after gun and superstructure were no more, and the torpedo-tubes pointed ridiculously to the skies.

The *Jackal* stood by and at dawn took off the wounded. At the same time the German bombers came in. It was just like a repeat of the *Kelly* affair six months earlier: a crippled ship far from home, the enemy circling above.

The only damage to the enemy occurred when Spitfire fighters appeared on the scene and shot down at short notice three of the bombers. Once again Mountbatten had to suffer the humiliation of being towed home – very slowly – by a tug; but in his usual sunny way, he appeared to have few regrets.* While two of his officers, Anthony Pugsley and Henry King, Captain of the *Kashmir*, considered the sudden turn to port disastrous, Mountbatten admitted only that he should perhaps have done it earlier in order to fire his torpedoes sooner.

No one was a greater admirer of Admiral Nelson than Mountbatten, but in this brief action he had attempted to revert to the old traditional parallel-line tactics rather than the radical piercing of the enemy line by single-line ahead attack, which had confused Admiral Villeneuve at Trafalgar and led to the great victory. And there was no Nelsonian 'Engage the enemy more closely' in Mountbatten's order, either.

In the official enquiries that followed this indisputable German victory against heavy odds, Commander Pugsley's view was upheld by the C-in-C Plymouth; while the Director of Trade and Staff Duties reported uncompromisingly: 'The night action organisation of the Flotilla does not appear to have been up to the required standard.' But no official rebuke was delivered and Mountbatten remained in command of the 5th Flotilla, simply shifting himself and his staff to other of his destroyers as required.

---

* When Chief of Defence Staff on a visit to Singapore, Mountbatten met Pugsley's son and remarked, 'Your father never forgave me for that night action in the *Javelin*.'

It was put out to the press that the action had been a British victory, although none of the three German destroyers had been touched. Churchill was so beguiled by the gallantry of Mountbatten's leadership that he invited him to Chequers at the weekend and, after congratulating him, actually offered him unprecedented promotion to the highly responsible post of Vice-Chief of Naval Staff. Mountbatten said later that he could hardly believe this offer, but replied, 'I would prefer to remain at sea and finish off their destroyers.' It seemed at the time, to some at least, that he was more likely to finish off his own destroyers. Instead, five weeks later and to his transparent delight, he was awarded the DSO he had pined for for so long. In his excitement he fancifully told Edwina that it was entirely because of her blue eyes. It was much more likely to have been brought about by Churchill's influence with Admiral Tovey, the new C-in-C Home Fleet.

Many years later, Pugsley recalled the final episode in that tow home:

> For the rest of that day and through half the following night, we made our painful way towards Plymouth Sound and, at about two o'clock the following morning, we passed the boom defences. Unable to secure to a buoy or to anchor, both ends of the ship being missing, we came to by getting one of the tugs secured alongside us to anchor. So for the rest of the night we lay in the Sound, sick at heart at our losses and the almost fatal wounds to the ship we had come to love so well, but deeply thankful to have survived and brought so much of her home.

8

The King Calls

s the *Javelin* went into dock for her complete rebuild,
up north at Hebburn, Hawthorn, Leslie were putting
the finishing touches to the rebuilt *Kelly*. She was
sorely needed, too. Britain's destroyer forces, more than
any other class of ship, were in the van of almost every
offensive and defensive operation. A big North Atlantic
convoy needed at least one flotilla and was lucky if it got
two destroyers. After a tremendous amount of pressure
on President Roosevelt, Churchill winkled fifty obsolete,
mass-produced, four-stacker, long laid-up destroyers out of
the US Navy. But it would still be many months before any
of them were fit for sea, and many of those who eventually
manned them claimed they never were fit for sea. Large
numbers of corvettes and other anti-submarine boats were
also under construction. Meanwhile, every destroyer was
worth her weight in gold.

Two days after Mountbatten had left one destroyer with
the repairers, he took the train north to see the *Kelly*. He
had succeeded, at last, in acquiring a pair of the much-
needed Oerlikons, which he had done so much to promote
and which greatly reinforced the *Kelly's* close anti-aircraft
fire-power. She was almost ready for sea, and within a
few more days would be able to accommodate her new

ship's company. Mountbatten was keen, perhaps too keen, to recover as many of his old crew as possible and had sent out a number of letters to them in the ships in which they were serving. This was not always looked on favourably by their new commanders, and led to a disappointing response. It turned out in the end that no fewer than 170 of the ship's total complement of 260 were 'green' youngsters, 'Hostilities Only' or 'HO's.

Mountbatten was horrified and complained to Edwina that more than half his men had been seasick the moment they left port. As soon as the numbers were complete he had the lower deck cleared and addressed them for the first time.

'I am not at all satisfied with the very large number of untrained, inexperienced men that Chatham have thought fit to send me,' he began. 'I want only real sailors who know their job and you new HOs will have to learn fast if you're going to stay with me. . . .' It was a very strong message and shocked a great number of them, but he also repeated his previous invigorating rallying-cries of 'keep on' and 'always steer for the guns'.

A number of the *Kelly*'s officers who had been on the first commission applied to serve under Mountbatten again, but Philip Burnett's place as first lieutenant was taken by Lord Hugh Beresford, a great-nephew of Admiral of the Fleet Lord Charles Beresford. The Beresfords were an Anglo-Irish family of ancient lineage and immoderate wealth. Lord Charles, a peppery, prejudiced and unamiable admiral, had initiated a vendetta against Mountbatten's father for his German origins during the First World War, which led to a rebuke from Churchill as First Lord of the Admiralty: 'The interests of the country do not permit the spreading of such wicked allegations by an officer of your rank. . . .'

Mountbatten had no need of misgivings about this young Beresford, a deeply religious, rather shy but thoroughly able officer. He had supervised the last stages of the *Kelly*'s rebuild and made himself popular with the Hawthorn, Leslie men. 'The chief impression he left on the working men here was of a lovable personality, who lived above the distinctions of class and creed,' wrote one.

Hugh Beresford was always ready to speak openly to the men on any subject, and his views about fear proved a great comfort to some of them. The worst part of fear, he used to tell them, whether it is of meeting people or of the dentist's drill or of bombs, is anticipation:

My faith in God has not prevented me from feeling fear but I find that God lifts fear from those who start by admitting that they are frightened. I have learned to be honest about my fears with another officer on the bridge or with the man who happens to be next to me. That opens the way for God to take charge again. What is more, it often helps the other fellow to get rid of his own fears.

All this was very different from Mountbatten's extrovertism and absolute fearlessness, but the blend of outlook of the two officers most responsible for the ship and her company was uniquely supportive and proved wonderfully rewarding.

Mountbatten was impatient to get to sea and initiate an intensive training programme, and was furious when he was thwarted. For the second time the *Kelly* could not even get out of the Tyne estuary without a mishap. At least they were steaming slowly this time when there was a misunderstanding over an order and the destroyer struck her brand new bows into the side of a merchantman, SS *Scorpion*. The dockyard maties could hardly believe their eyes, but it was back to work again on their accident-prone destroyer; luckily the damage was not too great.

Ten days before Christmas 1940, with her stem repaired, the *Kelly* left the yard yet again under her own steam and headed out to sea, carrying the prayers of the Hawthorn, Leslie dockyard maties for safe sailing, at least for a few weeks.

It did, however, become clear very quickly that this maiden voyage to Scapa Flow was not going to be free of incident. Soon after nightfall, with half the men still at the rails, their faces green or white, there were gun-flashes ahead. Mountbatten studied the flotilla exercises programme carried by every ship in the vicinity and there was no mention of gunnery practice. Fearing that these were German destroyers at work on coastal shipping, he was in something of a dilemma, even though his final decision was inevitable. With half his men prostrate, and in any case totally inexperienced at manning the guns – or anything else for that matter – there was every likelihood that they would be sunk in any close action.

'Always steer towards the sound of guns,' he had just told them, so what else could he do? The flash of firing continued, the *Kelly* was cleared for action, and it was not until they were within close range that the ship identified herself. She was indeed doing night gunnery practice, quite legitimately; it was just that no one had bothered to tell Mountbatten, or he had failed to pick up the message. But the incident sharpened everybody up and proved 'the best cure for *mal de mer*', as one of the old hands remarked.

By the time the *Kelly* reached Scapa Flow, Mountbatten and his officers had made some progress in sharpening up the crew. Two of Mountbatten's principles in working up a ship were to be prepared to lead by example and to keep the men interested. They were made aware of this early on. Beresford was attempting to instil more speed in the exercise of manning the ship's whaler at the davits, being lowered and pulling away to recover a lifebuoy thrown overboard. Five times these raw sailors failed to carry out their task in under four minutes. Mountbatten joined Beresford and learned of these dismal results. He immediately called for a volunteer crew from the officers to man the whaler and lower and raise it again after retrieving the lifebuoy. The operation was carried out swiftly and smoothly, and they had the lifebuoy on the deck in ninety seconds, amid the cheers of the men.

Gunnery drill in all calibres was carried out daily, and also in earnest, soon after their arrival in Scapa Flow. This was a prohibited area for flying, but one afternoon the distinctive sound of an aircraft engine was heard. The crews closed the guns with commendable speed as a single aircraft was seen coming towards them low over the water. The multiple .5s were the first to open fire, with such accuracy that the pilot was forced to bank steeply away, at the same time dropping the recognition flares of a 'friendly'. Still, they all felt the better for the sudden flow of adrenalin.

They were at sea again before Christmas, which became a moveable feast celebrated late between U-boat hunts in these cold and unwelcoming seas. The new HOs were becoming hardened to the wet and strenuous life on-board a destroyer in wartime, and seasickness had almost disappeared. At the Faeröe Islands, Mountbatten went ashore, leaving Beresford in command for a few days. He relished the responsibility, especially enjoying taking Sunday prayers, a service carried out rather perfunctorily by Mountbatten himself. The First Lieutenant intoned:

> Oh God, our loving Father, bless our efforts to make this ship efficient for your service. Help us to keep in mind the real causes of this war – dishonesty, greed, selfishness and lack of love – and to drive them out of the ship, so that she may be a pattern of the New World for which we are fighting. Bless also our homes and families. Give us the experience that there is no distance which cannot be bridged by your Holy Spirit if we open our hearts.

This went down very well. The sailors who had served in her before had at first missed the cheerful leadership of Philip Burnett, but they were now beginning to take to the more solemn Beresford and enjoyed giving of their best to him. When they heard from him the heartening news that they were leaving 'the frozen north' and heading for the English Channel, he was loudly cheered. Before they reached Plymouth they were joined by the *Kipling*, the *Kashmir* and the *Jersey*, completing 'The Fighting Fifth' once more. They doubled Land's End in heavy weather early on 18 January 1941 and sailed into Plymouth Sound that evening. They had now become part of the Western Approaches Striking Force, responsible for guarding this important area from U-boats as well as heavy German cruisers, the pocket battleship *Scheer*, and the battle-cruisers *Gneisenau* and *Scharnhorst*, now repaired after their damage in the Norwegian campaign.

With the use of French Atlantic bases close to the Allied convoy routes, these powerful surface forces were giving as much trouble as the U-boats. They ranged far into the South Atlantic and the Indian Ocean, using tanker-supply ships so that they could remain at sea for long periods. In harbour, the *Kelly* and her Flotilla were kept at two hours' notice for steam, and when the men could get ashore they were often brought back from the cinema by means of a notice flashed on the screen, and from pubs before they had got down their second pint. It was exhausting and exasperating work following up suspected sightings.

Mountbatten maintained the gung-ho spirit, one of his greatest qualities, although he did startle the men, and their officers, once when he made this announcement down the bridge voice-pipe:

We are now going to intercept the two battle-cruisers *Scharnhorst* and *Gneisenau* and also four cruisers of the 'Hipper' class, with destroyer screen. After breaking through the destroyer screen, we will torpedo the battle-cruisers and the cruisers, then will intercept the destroyers and hope to take one back as a prize to C-in-C Western Approaches. I know I can depend on each and every one of you.

This suicidal scenario was taken seriously and cheerfully by the ship's company. 'If he had said "*Kelly*'s got wings," and we were going to the North Pole, we'd have believed it, because everything he said, we always seemed to do it,' recalled one of the *Kelly*'s men.

The 5th Flotilla was ordered to intercept the two battle-cruisers on the assumption that they were heading for St Nazaire. Mountbatten would have none of that. He was convinced that they were going to Brest and infuriated his C-in-C by following his own hunch. He was then informed in no uncertain terms that if they escaped into St Nazaire, he would lose his command. But Mountbatten was right: the big German ships were docked in Brest by the time Mountbatten's destroyers reached the area. He was thus doubly lucky, because they would all certainly have been blown out of the water if they had met them at sea.

Mountbatten's second guess was that the *Hipper* had headed north, en route to Norway, and on his own initiative he turned north. On the second day, the weather got up and they were soon in the biggest storm the Irish Sea had experienced for many years. The little ships were thrown about as never before, and one wave hit the *Kelly* so that many of the crew thought she must capsize.

One able seaman told the author Kenneth Poolman:

Taff was bridge messenger and was busy hanging on to the side of the chart-table, when the sub-lieutenant sent him aft to fetch a towel and handkerchief from his cabin. Taff rolled his way along the sea side of the deck and dived into the ward-room flat just as a big sea showered the after tubes with white water. He got the articles and stuffed them inside his duffle-coat so as to have his hands free for gripping the lifeline on his return journey to the bridge. He came out of the after flat and turned round to put the clips on the door. He made the door fast and was just turning for'ard, when he saw a huge dark wave towering over the ship. He grabbed the rail running round the after flat and waited for the giant wave to hit him. There was a shattering roar. The whole ship disappeared and Taff was sucked off the rail and driven headlong through the sea. He hit the guardrail with a painful crash just as the ship started to roll back again. He picked himself up and staggered for'ard – to report to Subby that the wave had taken towel and handkerchief. 'And bloody nearly me with 'em,' said Taff under his breath.

The storm continued unabated into the evening when, just before darkness fell, another enormous wave struck the destroyer, rolling her over to starboard where she hung at seventy degrees. It seemed to everyone on deck and below that she must capsize, and when she at last righted herself it was like a sudden relief from physical pain. It took several more seconds for those on the bridge to note that the *Kelly* had paid a price after all. Her whaler and motor-boat had both been stripped from their davits and swept away. All the guardrails on the starboard side had also been ripped away along with the ship's carley rafts and the abandon-ship gear.

'All this would have been less irritating if we had not been the only ship that suffered damage, and the other ships expressed their amazement, touched with a bit of amusement,' recalled one of the *Kelly*'s officers. 'Fate was clearly not on our side. Luckily we did not have to return to Hawthorn, Leslie this time. The shame would have been too much to bear.'

Instead, with the rest of the Flotilla, the *Kelly* returned to Plymouth and went into the hands of the dockyard there. A week later and after some shore leave, she was able to resume her leadership of the Flotilla.

Mountbatten recorded:

It was about this time that we engaged in several minelaying escort operations, close in to French harbours, especially Brest where we hoped to lock in the *Gneisenau* and *Scharnhorst*. Our minelayer was the *Abdiel*, one of a class just built. Wisely, the Admiralty had given them massively powerful engines and they could steam nearly ten knots faster than we could.

'Destroyers think they are fast,' confirmed one of Mountbatten's men, 'but when the job was finished the *Abdiel* would lower her stern and leave the "ocean greyhounds" standing.'

The job of the 5th Flotilla was to counter any fire from shore batteries as they approached the area to be mined. The *Kelly* always took what Mountbatten called 'the place of honour' and his men called 'the place of suicide' on the landward side of the *Abdiel* as she laid her load through the stern shoots.

One night the *Kelly* found herself 'squeezed' almost into the outer harbour of Brest while her gun crews exchanged shots with the shore batteries at point-blank range. At dawn, when they were all racing for home, a *geschwader* of Stukas caught up with them. For the new HOs it was their first experience of being dive-bombed and they did not much care for it. But the twin Oerlikons greatly added to their fire-power at close range and none of the ships was hit, though there were several near misses.

After one of these night operations, Mountbatten announced over the loudspeakers that King George VI would be visiting them at 10.00 hours and that they would have three hours to clean the ship 'so you can shave in the paintwork'. The King was actually piped on-board soon after 10.30, and Mountbatten greeted his cousin warmly.

'It seems a long time since you were last on-board, sir,' Mountbatten said as he took him down to his cabin, which was less luxuriously fitted out than before.

'And meanwhile you've seen a great deal of action, Dickie.'

'Never been busier.' Over a pot of tea Mountbatten told the King about their night minelaying exploits.

The King later toured the ship, showing off his knowledge and familiarity learned long ago when he had served under the *nom de guerre* Lieutenant Johnson on-board the battleship *Collingwood* at the Battle of Jutland. Then he inspected the ship's company, all newly shaved and looking uncommonly smart.

'I'm very impressed,' he told Mountbatten. 'Impressed with everything I've seen. To mark the occasion, is it possible that everyone can have shore leave for the night?'

After thanking him, Mountbatten then took the King down to the ward-room, where lunch had been laid for him and all the *Kelly*'s officers.

'We talked about the war and almost nothing else,' Mountbatten recalled. 'Like his father, he loved talking Navy – *his* Navy, and always felt comfortable and at home on-board one of his ships. The shyness and diffidence seemed to disappear and he was just one of us. Again like his father, he would have loved to come to sea with us and see some action.'

A watch had to be maintained on-board that night, but it was the first time on this commission that all-night leave had been granted. Unfortunately, the wrong time had been chosen for a night's rest after beer, supper and a hot bath.

Early in the morning the German bombers came over and delivered a particularly vicious attack. The crew all wished that they were back in the *Kelly*, where at least they could man the guns and support the local anti-aircraft batteries. None of those on shore leave was hurt, but it was a shaking experience; it was also salutary to learn just what had been happening on the civilian front almost every night since the previous September.

Plymouth was still burning when they rejoined their ship. St Andrew's Church and Guildhall were nothing but rubble, and few buildings remained in Bedford and George Streets and Princess Square.

With the first hints of spring 1941 came the first flutters of evidence that Germany and Italy were about to open a new phase of the war. In Britain the winter bombing had been survived although at dreadful cost in lives and some cost to industry; at least it was clear that there was to be no invasion for the foreseeable future. While the U-boat war was being further intensified, and there remained the risk of German heavy ships, including the newly completed giant, *Bismarck*, breaking out and destroying Atlantic convoys, the centre-piece of war was shifting towards the eastern Mediterranean and the North African desert.

Hitler was intent on rapidly covering his flank before opening his mighty attack on the USSR – 'Operation Barbarossa' – by crushing Greece and Yugoslavia, weakening British naval power with the help of his Italian allies, and then driving the British Army out of Egypt. He had his eyes, as had the Kaiser in the First World War, on the oil-rich Middle East and the Soviet Union's under-belly.

All this, supported by intelligence from neutral Sweden and other sources, was pointing towards an attack on Russia.

In a memorandum of 14 April 1941 in connection with the need to cut German and Italian supply lines to North Africa, Churchill noted that Admiral Cunningham's fleet 'must be strengthened for the above purposes' and 'reinforcements of cruisers, minelayers and destroyers must be sent from the west as opportunity serves'.

With the benefit of hindsight it seems inconceivable that Mountbatten's 'Fighting Fifth' could have been omitted from these reinforcements to an area that was about to become the epicentre of the earthquake that was already rumbling in the east and the eastern Mediterranean.

PART THREE

THE FINAL BATTLE

9

'Terribly short of "air"'

ADMIRAL SIR DUDLEY POUND TO
ADMIRAL SIR ANDREW CUNNINGHAM

N ever in all its history had control of the Mediterranean been so delicately balanced as in the spring of 1941. The Mediterranean has been the scene of naval action for over five thousand years. The first ever ocean voyaging probably originated in Egypt around 3000 BC in boats developed from Nile papyrus vessels with a single lateen sail. Surviving detailed reliefs show Pharaoh Sahure's fleet of forty ships setting off to buy cedar for shipbuilding from Phoenicia, and there is evidence of military expeditions by sea not much later than this. More recent reliefs, around 1200 BC, show in remarkable detail the warships of the 'last great pharaoh', Ramses III, which fought against the Philistines of the Bible.

These early contests were no more than land battles at sea, with no weaponry in use to cripple enemy vessels. The first ship-destroying weapon was the ram, precursor of the gun, and then the torpedo. These deadly sharp prows were attached to the simple dugouts constructed by the Greeks also around 3000 BC. The ram was fitted to heavy warships right down to the Great War of 1914–18. In 1893 a British battleship manoeuvring in the Mediterranean accidentally struck the flagship with her ram, sending her to the bottom, with dreadful loss of life, in a few minutes, proving its continuing effectiveness as a weapon.

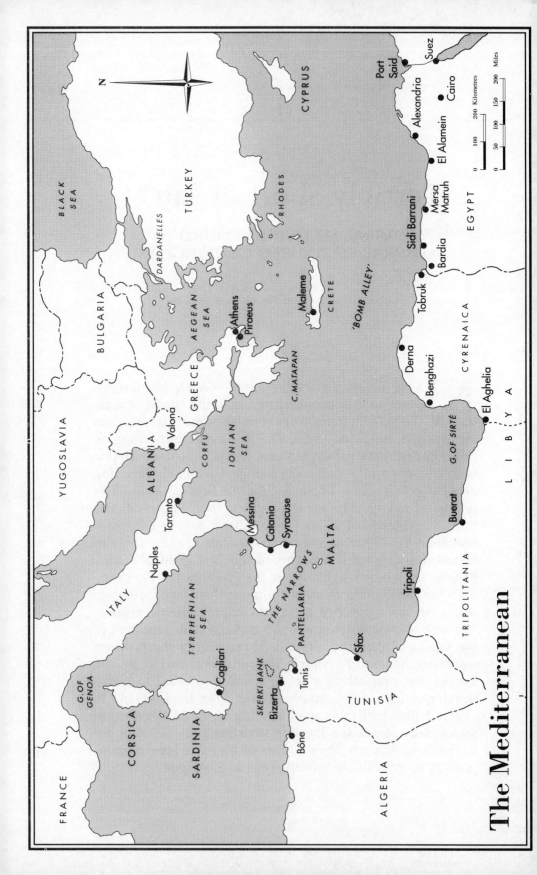

The Mediterranean

For centuries the chief vessel of war in the Mediterranean was the galley, rowed by slaves or volunteer oarsmen, which was still being built in the seventeenth century. By this time galleys had become remarkably sophisticated men o'war with up to 500 oarsmen and were armed with heavy cannon. The Spanish Armada of 1588 even included several giant galleys, or galleasses, but they could not stand up to the Bay of Biscay gales and were sent home. Like Mountbatten's destroyers, these Mediterranean galleys were highly manoeuvrable and were quick on acceleration and deceleration.

Venetians, Phoenicians, Genoese, Neapolitans and Greeks all used fighting galleys to protect their trade, and they were employed at the great Battle of Matapan as recently as 1717. But by this time the three-decker line-of-battleship was the queen of the Mediterranean, and the struggle for dominance and control of trade was fought out between the French, Dutch, Spanish and British at great naval actions like Palermo 1676 (French–Dutch), Malaga 1704 (English and Dutch–French and Spanish), Cape Passaro 1718 (English–Spanish), the Nile 1798 (French–British) and the Battle of Navarino 1827, the last to be fought exclusively under sail, with no fewer than five nations involved.

Action in the Mediterranean in the First World War was confined to U-boats, bombardment of the Dardanelles and counter-bombardment by the shore-based Germans and Turks, mining and counter-mining. The Royal Navy had held total control of the Mediterranean since Trafalgar in 1805 and remained the dominant force after 1918, although the Mediterranean Fleet, once Britain's premier fleet, had been superseded in importance by the Home and Channel Fleets since the dangerous expansion of the German Navy in the early years of this century.

In 1939 the French and Italians possessed modern fleets of roughly equal strength, while the British Mediterranean Fleet was marginally superior to both in material strength. Italian cruisers and destroyers were the most beautiful and fastest in the world, and fast modern battleships were being completed, but like the French the Italians had neglected their air-power, reckoning that their geographical situation made aircraft carriers unnecessary and leaving responsibility both for attack and defence in the air to the Italian Air Force. Because their ships were so lightly protected, it was clear that they were not designed for a gunnery slogging match. Their chief naval bases were at Taranto, Naples, Venice and Spezia.

The French Mediterranean Fleet's ships had been designed on the assumption that Italy would be the enemy in any future war. Their ships, too, were fast but not so swift as Italy's, while their all-round qualities were marginally superior. Their chief bases were Algiers, Oran, Toulon and Bizerta. Mountbatten, with his experience of them before the war, considered the French unreliable politically and unprepared for war.

The British C-in-C was Admiral Sir Andrew Cunningham, who had commanded the Mediterranean destroyers when Mountbatten had commanded the *Daring* and *Wishart*. Mountbatten had the highest opinion of him, which, alas, was not reciprocated. Later, Cunningham had been second-in-command in the Mediterranean (1937–8) and had succeeded Admiral Sir Dudley Pound when Churchill brought Pound back to become First Sea Lord at the outset of the war. Cunningham's promotion was ironically coincidental with the stripping of the Mediterranean Fleet of most of its ships, sorely needed at home. Admiral Tovey's destroyer force was reduced to five old Australian ships, and all that Cunningham himself was left with by November 1939 was three ancient light-cruisers, his flagship battleship *Warspite* having long since been transferred to home waters and the Norwegian fighting.

Hearing of the successful action against the *Admiral Graf Spee* off Montevideo and other actions 'in our quiet and almost peacetime routine . . . added greatly to our fretful impatience at being too much out of it', Cunningham complained. He did not have long to wait before he had all the action any commander could wish for. The Norwegian campaign, with its glorious destroyer actions and wretched losses, like the carrier *Glorious*, seemed from Malta to point to an imminent extension of the war. With every German success on land and sea, the attitude of Italy became increasingly suspect. 'There were ominous rumbles,' the Admiral reported, and learned to his relief that he was to get a fleet back, including the *Warspite*.

Three more battleships, albeit somewhat old and unmodernised, came under Cunningham's command. 'The prospect of again having a deck beneath one's feet was most exhilarating,' Cunningham noted. The French, too, seemed at last to be taking the situation seriously and, as a political gesture aimed at Italy, despatched a powerful force through the Mediterranean to the British base at Alexandria. Cunningham received another battleship, modern cruisers and destroyers, and on 11 May thankfully hoisted his flag again in the modernised *Warspite*, 'and very glad indeed we all were to be back in our old quarters. I think the men were glad to see us also. There is a cachet about being fleet flagship which extends to the most junior rating on-board.'

The Mediterranean Fleet lacked one arm, with ominous implications for the future: air-power. No carrier could be spared from home waters for the present, and the RAF had almost nothing at Malta and was desperately weak in Egypt, where the powerful Italian Army in Libya was likely to strike as soon as war was declared.

From the Admiralty, Dudley Pound wrote to Cunningham,

> I am afraid you are terribly short of 'air', but there again I do not see what can be done because, as you will realise, every available aircraft is wanted in home waters. The one lesson we have learned here is that it is essential to have fighter protection over the fleet whenever they are within range of enemy bombers. You will be without such protection, which is a very serious matter, but I do not see any way of rectifying it.

Unfortunately not everyone, including the Prime Minister, had learned that lesson, and it was to be a most expensive failure costing many ships and many thousands of lives.

Meanwhile, Cunningham did what he could, and was blessed by – for the present – having to deal with only the amazingly inefficient Italian Air Force, the *Regia Aeronautica*. At Malta, heavily bombed from the first day of the Italian declaration of war on 11 June 1940, three Gloster Gladiator biplane fighters were discovered in crates; they were hastily put together and flown by flying-boat pilots with great verve and some success against the Italian bombers.

At last, some weeks after Dudley Pound's lamentation about 'air', Cunningham received the old carrier *Eagle*, with a complement of 'Stringbags', the Navy's standard torpedo-reconnaissance bomber, the Swordfish. Both the Italians and the Germans mocked the biplane Swordfish with her configuration not unlike that of a 1914–18 plane. Flying into a strong wind, the Swordfish could scarcely keep up with an Italian destroyer or cruiser, and on one occasion was outpaced by a margin. Nevertheless, she was loved by her crews of two, and both the German and Italian Navies had reason to regret the plane's versatility and 'sting'. Her first value to Cunningham, who knew he could never catch the Italian fleet in retreat, was to torpedo the enemy from the air and hope to slow him up.

Cunningham was also conscious of a desperate shortage of submarines, compared with the fleet of some one hundred operated by Italy. However, after an early success in sinking an old British cruiser, Italian submarines made few sinkings and appeared to be as poorly commanded as the bombers.

Cunningham listened to the news from Europe with increasing dismay, culminating in the collapse of France on 24 June 1940. This transformed the balance of naval power in the Mediterranean, with the added danger that some of the French Navy would turn themselves over to their conquerors. There was a strong French naval force at Alexandria, under the command of Vice-Admiral R. E. Godfroy, a most charming and reasonable man – reasonable enough, under mild *force majeure*, to agree after much anxious negotiation to one of Cunningham's alternative proposals, in effect to put his ships in a condition in which they could not go to sea.

At the other end of the Mediterranean, the main force including modern battle-cruisers was at Oran when news of the surrender came through. Admiral Sir James Somerville, at Gibraltar, was ordered to take a powerful force including a modern carrier and HMS *Hood*, the biggest warship in the world, to a position off Oran and attempt to negotiate, as Cunningham was doing at Alexandria. Here the French C-in-C was more obdurate and refused all alternatives, with the regretful result that the French ships were shelled and bombed at their moorings with terrible loss of life. The French never forgave this 'act of barbarism', and Churchill wept in the House of Commons when he announced the outcome, absolutely necessary though it was.

Aside from Cunningham's relief from anxiety at this neutralisation of French naval forces in the Mediterranean, the Oran bombardment had enormous political implications. In the days before the air Battle of Britain gave Germany her first major defeat, many Americans had written off any chance of British survival against the all-conquering Germans. Oran showed that Britain and her Empire meant business. The Spanish dictator, General Franco, poised on a knife-edge of indecision whether to throw in his lot with Hitler, was deeply impressed by the British firmness and procrastinated about German requests to allow a German force to attack Gibraltar from Spain and set up a base in the Canary Islands. Either would have been disastrous to the British cause.

The Mediterranean military and naval situation was difficult enough in the summer of 1940 without having to deal with threats from Germany adding to those from Mussolini's Italy, already poised with superior forces to advance into Egypt and capture the all-important naval base at Alexandria. There was every likelihood of an Italian attack on Greece, too, and as a contingency arrangement the British Chiefs of Staff planned to occupy Crete to safeguard the eastern Mediterranean.

At sea Cunningham by August was further reinforced by modern cruisers and the new armoured carrier *Illustrious*, which had naval fighters as well as Swordfish. The Admiral felt reasonably satisfied with his strength, especially as the Italians showed no inclination to fight. Malta was made more secure with reinforced anti-aircraft power, and a squadron of modern Hurricane fighters was flown off an old carrier and landed safely on the island.

Cunningham had been much disturbed by the hectoring instructions from the Admiralty, inspired of course by Churchill, to take up a more offensive stance. No British admiral was more imbued with a spirit of aggression than Andrew Cunningham. His difficulty was, like Admiral Jellicoe's in the First World War, to get the enemy to come out and fight. But Cunningham had already planned to attack the Italian fleet in harbour if it would not face action at sea. His proposal, to the First Sea Lord in London, was to fly off a mixed force of bombers and torpedo-bombers from his two carriers at night and destroy the Italian battle fleet in their main base at Taranto.

The success of the operation had to depend on air reconnaissance by the RAF from Malta to ensure that there were enough warships in the harbour to warrant the attack. This became possible when the RAF received some American-built Maryland twin-engine aircraft, which could fly high enough and fast enough to evade Italian fighters. This interservice part of the operation worked excellently. The *Illustrious* despatched a plane to Malta to pick up the latest photographs, from which it was seen that there were five battleships in the Mar Grande, the heavily protected harbour at Taranto. At almost the last moment, a final reconnaissance flight observed a sixth battleship entering the harbour. 'So all the pheasants had gone home to roost,' Cunningham remarked with satisfaction.

The old *Eagle* developed trouble, so the *Illustrious* alone took part, despatching twenty-one Swordfish in two waves, the first at 8.35 p.m. on the evening of 11 November 1940. There was a three-quarter moon and a layer of thin cloud at 8,000 feet. The planes had long-range tanks and were expected back – it was hoped – in some six hours' time. They were the most extraordinary six hours in the history of the Fleet Air Arm. An ex-FAA pilot, Hugh Popham, has written:

The first wave of Swordfish approached the sleeping harbour and the flare-droppers were detached. They flew along the line of the eastern mole, their flares blossoming behind them and illuminating the ships, the harbour and the moored balloons. As the first guns opened up and the flare-droppers banked and dived to bomb the inner harbour, the first sub-flight of torpedo aircraft crept in low over the water and into a wall of gunfire.

Cunningham later said, 'The zeal and enthusiasm with which these deliberate and accurate attacks were carried out in comparatively slow aircraft in the face of intense fire cannot sufficiently be praised.' He concluded, 'The results were devastating. Photographs taken the following day showed two of the battleships beached, one resting on the bottom and a fourth sunk by the bows, with further damage to a cruiser and destroyers.'

'It was as if we had lost a great naval battle, and could not foresee being able to recover from the consequences,' wrote the Italian official historian. At a cost of two aircraft and their crews, the balance of naval power in the Mediterranean now rested with the Royal Navy.

The lesson was taken to heart by the Imperial Japanese Navy and led to the conception of its attack on Pearl Harbor little more than a year later. 'I was about to recommission the *Kelly* at the time the news came through,' Mountbatten remembered. 'Of course I was thrilled to bits like everyone else, but it didn't entirely surprise me. At the time of the Abyssinian crisis in 1935 Admiral Ramsay [Commanding Aircraft Carriers] worked out a scheme using a couple of carriers flying Baffins with torpedoes and bombs to deal with the Italian fleet in Taranto. They even set up a refuelling base in Greece somewhere. Those were the days before long-range tanks.'

The idea was revived by Dudley Pound when he was C-in-C Mediterranean in 1938, and now at his desk at the Admiralty, he reported to Cunningham, 'Just before the news of Taranto the Cabinet was rather down in the dumps; but the news of Taranto had a most amazing effect upon them.' Churchill could no longer accuse the Admiral of being unaggressive.

As a captain who had already seen the effects of dive-bombing on ships, including the *Bison* and *Gurkha* off Norway, the success of Taranto served to confirm Mountbatten's belief that only air-cover could save surface ships in the face of torpedoing or bombing.

Two weeks before Taranto, the Italian Army had invaded Greece, as expected. The British responded as planned and occupied the island of Crete, with its useful naval anchorage at Suda Bay covering the eastern Mediterranean. To this new ally, Britain now sent in a small force of fighters and torpedo-bombers to harass Italian supply ships. And to the astonishment of the world, fighting over a terrain they knew so well the Greeks threw the Italians back into Albania whence they had come.

The Italian Army under Marshal Graziani, which had penetrated some distance into Egypt early in the war, was no more successful when General Wavell opened his first offensive early in December 1940. As in Greece, the Italians were far more numerous, but Wavell drove relentlessly forward, capturing one after another of the coastal towns, culminating in Benghazi on 6 February. He also captured tens of thousands of prisoners, who, when shipped back to England, made useful farmworkers for the rest of the war. Throughout this advance, Cunningham had co-operated with Wavell by delivering forward supplies and intercepting Italian convoys across the Mediterranean. As Wavell's motor transport was inadequate, he was almost totally dependent on these sea-delivered supplies to maintain his advance and then hold his positions.

In the early weeks of 1941, then, the Mediterranean Fleet was allowed a breathing-space. Convoys to Malta got through safely, Italian convoys to North Africa suffered severely. Malta's defences had been greatly strengthened, and bombers operating from the island were regularly bombing enemy ports on the mainland of Italy and Tripoli in North Africa.

Adolf Hitler, while no appreciator of sea-power, was forced to recognise that his partner was in danger of total defeat in North Africa, had been defeated in Greece and had lost control of the eastern Mediterranean. In the past he had offered Mussolini support, but national pride was at stake and the Italian dictator was loath to demonstrate publicly that, with his superior forces on land, sea and air, he still could not match up to the British Empire. South African troops had cleared the Italian forces out of Kenya, British troops had entered Italian Somaliland and there was a pro-British uprising in Abyssinia.

Hitler realised that something had to be done to bail out his partner. He was fretting to open his spring attack on Russia and considered anything else a sideshow. Nevertheless, Greece had to be subjugated, General Wavell rolled back to Egypt, and Cairo and Alexandria occupied.

Early in the New Year 1941, a new shape was seen in the skies over Malta and the eastern Mediterranean, and a new uniform identified among the sands of North Africa. Hitler had decided to form an Afrika Korps to put some steel into the Italian Army, and a powerful unit, named *Fliegerkorps X*, equipped with the most modern fighters and bombers, was despatched first to Sicily and later to Greece. Hitler also strongly reinforced his U-boats in the Mediterranean. All three German services were now to have a profound effect on the situation.

The Italians with their high-level bombers in immaculate formation had bombed Malta time and again, and had done much damage though, with the arrival of Hurricanes, at high cost. Their bombing at sea had had few successes. Time and again Cunningham's ships sailed through forests of water spouts from exploding bombs and were rarely hit. With the arrival of Ju 87 Stukas in great numbers, formidable Ju 88s and Me 109 fighters – all battle-hardened from Scandinavia, France and the Battle of Britain – it was a very different story.

The shock effect of the first sighting of Stukas in the Mediterranean was well told by Cunningham himself after observing the sufferings of his only carrier, the *Illustrious*, which only a brief time earlier had made possible the crippling of Italy's battle fleet.

Large formations of aircraft were sighted to the northward, and were very soon overhead. They were recognised as German, three squadrons of Stukas. The *Illustrious* flew off more fighters; but neither they nor the patrol already in the air could gain sufficient height to do anything. We opened up with every AA [anti-aircraft] gun we had as one by one the Stukas peeled off into their dives, concentrating almost the whole venom of their attack upon the *Illustrious*. At times she became almost completely hidden in a forest of great bomb splashes.

One was too interested in this new form of dive-bombing attack really to be frightened, and there was no doubt we were watching complete experts. . . . The attacks were pressed home to point-blank range, and as they pulled out of their dives some of them were seen to fly along the flight deck of the *Illustrious* below the level of her funnel.

The carrier had taken six direct hits with 250 kg. bombs, crippling her steering and forcing her to circle helplessly at low speed. Casualties were very heavy and the flight deck was unusable. Any unarmoured carrier would have been at the bottom, but the *Illustrious* was able to limp into Malta harbour, where she was hit again.

This was the Stukas' first victim in the Mediterranean. There were to be many more. The German campaigns in Greece, Crete and North Africa were entirely dependent on smooth-flowing supplies, and these supply lines were largely by sea, almost wholly so in the case of North Africa. For this reason the neutralisation of Cunningham's fleet was essential. The Germans would do what they could with their U-boats, and these became increasingly effective, culminating in the sinking of the modern carrier *Ark Royal* off Gibraltar and the battleship *Barham* at the other end of the Mediterranean. And by early March 1941 the Luftwaffe had formed a complete *Luftflotte* of some eight hundred aircraft under the command of Field Marshal Kesselring, operating mainly from Sicily and Greece.

But the German High Command was becoming increasingly resentful at the failure of the Italian Navy to take any useful part in these operations. Its record was certainly a sorry one and its strategy seemed to be to maintain a 'fleet in being' as a threat rather than committing forces to battle. At last, towards the end of March, the German High Command managed to extract some sort of commitment out of the Italian Admiralty, partly by deception. '*Fliegerkorps X*, in an attack on the port of Alexandria, bombed and knocked out of action two British battleships,' ran a false German claim calculated to persuade Admiral Angelo Iachino, the Italian C-in-C, that the odds in his favour were even greater than they actually were.

Finally, he left the protection of his base. In a long and confused action, partly at night and even by day in poor visibility for much of the time because of smoke-screens laid by both sides, the Italians lost three of their heavy-cruisers and two destroyers in a night gun battle, with no casualties on the British side. In a valiant torpedo-plane attack, the brand new Italian battleship *Vittorio Veneto* was struck and slowed to sixteen knots. This might have been Cunningham's chance to finish her off, but luck was not on his side, and the Italian Admiral managed to elude his pursuers.

It remained a fine victory, and the Battle of Cape Matapan greatly cheered the British fleet – and all those at home – as it was to diminish almost to extinction the Italian fighting spirit.

It was almost the only cheerful news from the Mediterranean for many months. The German 12th Army of eleven divisions plus four armoured divisions marched into southern Yugoslavia and Greece on the morning of 6 April. All through the long winter the Greeks, with almost no transport and few modern weapons, had held off the Italians. Now they had the support of strong British, Australian and New Zealand troops, eager for action and supported by some eighty RAF fighters and bombers. But it was only a matter of time, and not much of it, before the combined forces were in full retreat south, shelled and bombed from the air. There were courageous holding actions among the mountains and passes, especially by the 5th New Zealand Brigade at the Olympus pass, but with the almost total loss of RAF strength there was as little air support as in Norway.

The Greek Government sued for peace on 24 April, and the priority now was to rescue as many British and Commonwealth troops as possible. 'We were now confronted with another of those evacuations by sea which we had endured in 1940,' wrote Churchill. 'This was Namsos over again, and on ten times the scale.' And with many more than ten times the casualties. The Junkers bombers were everywhere, mercilessly bombing and machine-gunning the troops as they awaited rescue, and then setting about the ships in which they got away. One overloaded transport was sunk at dawn, and the two destroyers who rescued most of the 700 men from the water were in turn dive-bombed and sunk. Only fifty survived.

Some fifty thousand troops, including RAF personnel, were taken off, with around twelve thousand men wounded or made prisoner; 18,850 of those rescued were evacuated to Crete and remained there as reinforcements for the further battle ahead. 'We shall aid and maintain the defence of Crete to the last,' Churchill signalled Wavell on 17 April 1941.

It was an island that was to figure so critically in the service of HMS *Kelly* and the life of her Captain, now at Malta, awaiting 'the brazen throat of war'.

10

'Prolific in air'

ADMIRAL CUNNINGHAM TO THE ADMIRALTY
ON THE LUFTWAFFE'S STRENGTH

I f anyone in high command still doubted that air-power dominated sea-power without adequate air defence, they had only to read reports from the Mediterranean and Malta in the late spring of 1941. The 5th Flotilla,* in company with their old friend the minelayer *Abdiel* and light-cruiser *Dido*, were made aware of this as they approached Malta from Gibraltar. And the fact that there were thousands of spectators on the battlements of Grand Harbour to celebrate their safe arrival seemed to suggest that they had gained some triumph in surviving the dangers from the Sicily-based Stukas.

'When I saw the terrible bomb damage in Valetta and the wrecks in the harbour,' recalled Mountbatten, 'my mind went back to those happy days with the *Daring* and *Wishart* in the 1930s, and the polo and the parties ashore and of course Edwina and Patricia and Pammy [his daughters]. It was all Navy family life at its best, and a great contrast with now.'

A raid by seventy bombers came over soon after the Flotilla docked in Grand Harbour, the docks and the new

---

* All the destroyers had exchanged their aftermost set of torpedo-tubes for a four-inch anti-aircraft gun. Only the *Kelly* had Oerlikons.

arrivals being the primary target. 'This was something we just had to get used to, like everyone else here,' Mountbatten continued. 'When it was over I went ashore and met George Simpson [Commander George ("Shrimp") Simpson, commanding Mediterranean submarines], who explained that all ships' companies except those manning the guns should be ashore in the shelters when there was a raid.'

According to Simpson himself it was not quite as straightforward as this. Simpson had been ordered to visit Mountbatten with the necessary charts and show him 'where the best hunting grounds are'. After a long bicycle ride (no staff cars) in the burning heat, he found the *Kelly* at Parlatorio Wharf and went on-board just as the sirens sounded. 'The one place not to be in a raid was on a warship, and it was clear that the enemy were well aware of the 5th Flotilla's recent arrival. . . .'

The Quartermaster explained that Mountbatten would soon be back; meanwhile, perhaps, Simpson would make himself comfortable in Mountbatten's cabin.

'But I wasn't a bit comfortable,' Simpson recalled. 'Ten minutes had gone since the warning. . . . What the hell was I doing here anyway? What possible use could I be to my submarines when dead?'

Simpson held on for a few minutes longer and decided to seek shelter ashore. He was intercepted by Mountbatten. After exchanging greetings and a good look at the sky, Mountbatten said, 'They tell me over the telephone that the raid is 'seventy plus'. What exactly does that mean?'

'It means that at least seventy bombers and accompanying fighters are on their way.'

'Under these circumstances, what do you do?' Mountbatten then asked, and was told that they all ran for the shelters.

'I suggest you and I take shelter now, sir,' Simpson replied.

But Mountbatten would not shift 'one inch', not until a stick of bombs fell a short distance away, and then 'we walked to the shelter'.

Later, Mountbatten took a more circumspect view. 'Except for our brief brush with the Germans at Namsos,' he recounted, 'we had not seen aerial warfare on this scale before. The

Germans and Italians bombed Malta night and day. I saw no point in risking the *Kelly*'s entire company, so I sent half the Flotilla's companies ashore to the shelters every night, and the other half manned the guns. I stayed on-board every night. A fine story it would have made if the *Kelly* had been sunk with Captain Mountbatten skulking in an air-raid shelter! But in all my life I've never been so scared.'

To his old polo-playing friend, Robert Neville, Mountbatten wrote, 'On average we have four daylight air-raids and two night raids. About sixty aircraft come over the Grand Harbour together, bombs whistle down, and all of us have had many narrow shaves. . . .'

Like many naval officers, Mountbatten held the RAF responsible for this continuous harassment from the air, ignoring the fact that there was only a handful of Hurricanes, most of them old Mark Is, to meet these raids which were heavily escorted by Me 109 fighters. It particularly enraged Mountbatten that German minelaying aircraft seemed to be able to magnetic mine the approaches to Valetta harbour with impunity, restricting the passage of his ships in and out.

His fury increased when, five days after their arrival, the *Jersey* was blown up by one of these mines, her wreck completely blocking the entrance.

Mountbatten signalled a note of complaint to the Vice-Chief of Naval Staff, Vice-Admiral Sir Tom Phillips, at the Admiralty, pointing out that there was not even a sweeper to deal with the mines since the last one had been put out of action. He also complained to Admiral Cunningham at Alexandria, saying how much he hated the circumstances in which his Flotilla was existing. This cavilling was very un-Mountbatten-like and Cunningham was clearly surprised by the complaint. But he did his best to cheer him up, agreed that it was hell for any warship's company at Malta and promised he would bring the Flotilla to Alexandria as soon as he could, 'though I warn you there is no rest for destroyers in the Mediterranean'.

Cunningham's Fleet Torpedo Officer devised an ingenious method of clearing the mines and recommended it to the Vice-Admiral Malta. 'He was directed to blast a channel into

Malta with depth-charges, of which, fortunately, there were plenty in store. . . . The basis of the idea was that a depth-charge dropped every so many yards would counter-mine or upset the firing mechanism of any magnetic mine in the vicinity of the explosion.' It worked like a dream.

The reason why Cunningham wanted the 5th Flotilla to remain at Malta for as long as possible was the urgent need to attack Rommel's supply lines across the Mediterranean. Wavell's desert army had been much weakened by the withdrawal of troops and supplies to help defend Greece, and later Crete. Rommel, meanwhile, was being reinforced and receiving supplies from Italy, and seriously threatening Egypt.

To Cunningham, Churchill had emphasised the importance of intercepting these supplies. On 1 May he signalled,

> Above all we look to you to cut off seaborne supplies from the Cyrenaican ports and to beat them up to the utmost. It causes grief here whenever we learn of the arrival of precious aviation spirit [to the enemy] in one ship after another.

He added,

> This great battle for Egypt is what the Duke of Wellington called 'a close-run thing', but if we can reinforce you by Operations 'Tiger' and 'Jaguar' [tank and air reinforcements], and you can cut off the tap of inflow, our immense armies in the Middle East will soon resume their ascendancy.

The mere presence of the 5th Flotilla at Malta was a discouragement to the German–Italian convoys. When these were spotted by air from Malta, Mountbatten would lead out the *Kelly* and the others and more often than not the convoy would return to base. Then, on the night of 10–11 May 1941, Mountbatten was ordered to intercept a convoy heading for Benghazi, and follow this up with a bombardment of the shipping inside the harbour.

The operation was not a great success. The convoy was not found, though he did damage a merchantman close to the entrance to the harbour. It was a brilliant moonlit night, but by a piece of faulty navigation the destroyers overshot the position from which they could best carry out their shoot. One report ran:

> As it appeared that the Flotilla had not yet been discovered by the enemy, the Captain decided to make a short leg to seaward. As soon as the Flotilla was reformed on the correct line of bearing they turned in again at twelve knots. When the exact position was reached, all guns opened fire on the shipping inside the harbour, now clearly seen against the light.

There was, however, doubt about how much damage they inflicted as most of the shipping appeared to be already damaged beyond repair. The defending guns opened fire as they increased speed to thirty knots and left this dangerous area. A short time later the horribly familiar sound of Stuka engines could be heard, and the crews manned the anti-aircraft guns. To dive-bomb at night seemed ludicrously dangerous, but this is what the skilful German pilots did, coming down at their usual steep angle, the moonlight flashing on their wings.

The 5th Flotilla ships dodged and swerved, threw out smoke floats and fired away with their light guns. No one was hit, and it was perhaps with equal relief on both sides when the Junkers made off back towards Africa.

It is some 380 miles from Benghazi to Malta, and it was not until midday that the chunky silhouette of Malta showed up ahead. 'It was like going back to prison after being let out for a while,' one of Mountbatten's men commented. 'And the warders were a rough lot.' In fact, there was an air-raid in progress as they approached the marked channel through the mines the Germans had laid. 'They must have been disappointed to find us missing.'

They were back at their old berths in the early afternoon, the *Kelly* as usual in the dock recently vacated by the *Illustrious*, which was on her way to the United States via Suez for repairs.

At Alexandria, Cunningham studied the reports of the raid

and was not best pleased. He signalled the First Sea Lord in London:

> I was a little disappointed with the 5th Flotilla. They were dive-bombed by moonlight and legged to the Northward. If they had gone South in accordance with their orders I think they would have picked up four ships which arrived at Benghazi the next day.

This was Mountbatten's last operation from Malta. A few days later, 'The Fighting Fifth' received orders to leave Malta, not for the comfort and relative security of Alexandria but for the most dangerous part of the eastern Mediterranean.

The critical battles for Greece and Crete in the spring and early summer of 1941 were marked by individual courage and resourcefulness, fine leadership, weak planning and preparation, a dreadful dearth of supplies and equipment, and above all the almost total dominance of air-power – German air-power because the British–Australasian forces had virtually none. Only in sea-power did the Allies dominate, and this was thanks to the lame leadership of the Italian Navy, which remained powerful only on paper.

So strong had been the pressure on General Wavell, especially after the arrival of Rommel and his Afrika Korps and the necessity of coming to the aid of Greece, that a long-planned invasion and conquest of the Italian island of Rhodes with its fine airfields had been postponed time and again. Now Crete was the last island base available in the eastern Mediterranean, 'a vital outpost of Egypt and Malta,' as Churchill defined it. It is a rocky, mountainous island of 3,200 square miles, difficult fighting country, with deep valleys and peaks rising to around seven thousand feet. The northern coast especially, facing Greece and therefore the most vulnerable, is heavily indented, and a strong force with ample time to prepare defences was needed to hold off any invasion. Neither was available.

Nor was there any 'plan or drive' evident in the six months since Crete was first occupied. 'The responsibility for the defective study of the problem [of defence] and for the feeble execution of the directions given must be shared between Cairo and Whitehall,' Churchill later concluded. The need to provide landing facilities from the sea on the south side of the island, and the building of a road to the vital anchorage of Suda Bay, had not even begun.

It was not numbers of defending troops that the Crete command lacked. There were already over 28,000 men there before the evacuation of Greece, and a further 5,300 British, 6,400 New Zealand and 7,000 Australian soldiers arrived to swell the ranks when Greece fell. Nor was their morale low. They had in the New Zealand general, Sir Bernard Freyberg VC, an outstanding leader of unquestioned courage who had been wounded so often in the First World War that he had lost count.*

Wavell, Freyberg's senior officer in Cairo, was optimistic about the outlook at the end of April. 'I am assuming that Crete will be held,' he signalled. But Freyberg, a realist as well as a singularly determined soldier, after studying the defences at his disposal, reported doubtfully on the island's ability to hold out. He signalled Wavell on 1 May:

> Forces at my disposal are totally inadequate to meet attack envisaged. Unless fighter aircraft are greatly increased and naval forces made available to deal with seaborne attacks I cannot hope to hold out with land forces alone, which as result of campaign in Greece are now devoid of any artillery, have insufficient tools for digging, very little transport, and inadequate war reserves of equipment and ammunition. Force here can and will fight, but without full support from Navy and Air Force cannot hope to repel invasion.

There was no likelihood, nor even possibility, of receiving more RAF support before the expected German invasion took place. In fact, the few remaining planes, survivors of

---

* In the 1920s while staying in the same country house together, Churchill asked to see his wounds. Freyberg stripped, and they counted twenty-seven scars and gashes. But Freyberg did not regard that as a true figure, because 'you nearly always get two wounds for every bullet or splinter, because they mostly have to go out as well as to go in'.

the Greek campaign, were flown away to Egypt rather than be massacred on the ground.

Three days before Freyberg's dismal report was received in Cairo, the Joint Intelligence Committee in London wrote an appreciation which was not made immediately available to him for fear that it would add to the pessimism in the Crete command. This predicted an attack preceded by heavy bombing from Greek airfields and from Rhodes before the arrival of air- and seaborne troops, the former comprising up to four thousand in the first strike alone.

The German Air Corps had received a tremendous amount of publicity before and in the early months of the war. During the British invasion scare of the summer of 1940, parachutists in great numbers were daily – and nightly – expected, followed by the warning sound of church bells ringing throughout the land. They had never come because the RAF retained control of the skies of southern Britain. Now this *corps d'élite* could enjoy total domination of the sky, and was known to be in the Balkans.

But there was no doubt that General Freyberg would receive 'the full support' of the Royal Navy. 'It is now necessary to fight hard for Crete, which seems soon to be attacked heavily,' Churchill informed Cunningham on 1 May. It was hardly a necessary warning. In gallant attempts to run supplies through to Crete from Egypt, half the field guns and engineer field stores Freyberg desperately needed were sunk en route to the island, and of fifteen supply ships which eventually reached Suda Bay eight were sunk or seriously damaged in the harbour.

The stress and strain of unremitting pressure on Cunningham's officers and men were beginning to show, and the damage to and loss of ships were already serious.

We had hoped for a respite for our cruisers and destroyers after the gruelling time they had had during the evacuation of Greece and for the weeks before that [wrote Cunningham]. There was hardly one of them which was not in urgent need of repair or refit, and, above all, of rest for the ships' companies.

In a memorandum to the First Sea Lord, Cunningham wrote of the 'signs of strain among the officers and ratings, particularly in the anti-aircraft cruisers and also in the destroyers . . . never a trip to sea without being bombed'.

In the midst of all these travails, the Mediterranean Fleet had other supply problems on its hands. Churchill, in answer to urgent appeals from Wavell, had determined to take the grave risk of passing a convoy ('Tiger') of fast merchantmen, loaded with over three hundred tanks, through the Mediterranean, saving the long passage round the Cape. Wavell had learned of a large consignment of German tanks reaching Rommel, and he feared a powerful and perhaps overwhelming attack in late May.

Force H at Gibraltar would cover this convoy as far as the Sicilian Narrows. South of Malta, Cunningham himself would take over, at the same time escorting to Malta sorely needed supplies, especially of oil. Fortune certainly favoured the brave on this occasion. At the rendezvous of the two fleets, the weather unprecedentedly was misty with low cloud, and later the few slight interventions from the air were driven off by the carrier *Formidable*'s fighters and anti-aircraft fire.

The success of 'Tiger' was a turning-point in the desert war, underlining not only the interdependence of the fighting forces but also the value of playing for high stakes when it seems necessary. It was certainly a great relief to Cunningham as he prepared himself and his fleet for the inevitable coming struggle in Cretan waters.

The German Air Corps, that élite body of airborne infantry, part paratroops, part glider-borne, was made up of young men, mostly one-time Hitler Youth, fanatically loyal to Hitler and the Fatherland, trained to the highest degree and aching for action. British intelligence watched them closely, and when they moved south from Germany, Churchill feared that they would be used in an attack on Malta. It is one of the unsolved mysteries of the war why they did not do so. Judged on their performance later, they would have had little trouble in occupying and holding the island, which would have been a savage blow to the Allied cause.

With the German conquest of Greece, the German Air Corps was known to have moved into that country. In fact, they had been waiting restlessly to attack Crete ever since the Allies had occupied it. The island was a perfect target for their special skills, and since 'Operation Mercury' was authorised on 21 April, under the command of General Löhr, it had been planned in the closest detail. It was expected that the Air Corps would rapidly capture one of the three main airfields on the island so that reinforcements could be flown in, and that as soon as a port was captured massive seaborne reinforcements would follow. There was no shortage of shipping, nor of power in the air. There were in Greece over 300 long-range bombers and 250 Ju 87 Stukas, 270 Me 109s and some 50 twin-engine Me 110s, besides transport planes.

General Freyberg planned his defence to meet just this scenario, neither General taking into account that Cunningham's powerful fleet might intervene to block sea reinforcements.

The German attack began at dawn on 20 May with a ferocious bombing of the defences of Maleme airfield. Wave after wave of Junkers and Heinkel bombers pinpointed the anti-aircraft and artillery positions in the area of Maleme for an hour, coming down low after their bombing run and strafing with machine-gun fire.

The bombardment was still going on when the first formations of Ju 52 tri-motors came in low amid the puffs of exploding shells from the few surviving anti-aircraft guns. At about five hundred feet the paratroopers streamed out of the fuselage doors, their parachutes blossoming out a second or two later so that for a moment the sky seemed filled with swinging white circles like meadow daisies in a breeze. The whole battalion landed between Canea and Maleme airfield, immediately formed into groups and went into the attack with their light weapons.

A complete German regiment was soon on the ground – those who were not killed in their descent – and being attacked with tremendous ferocity by the 5th New Zealand Brigade, who were in turn bombed and machine-gunned from the air. But the day's fighting had not yet reached the

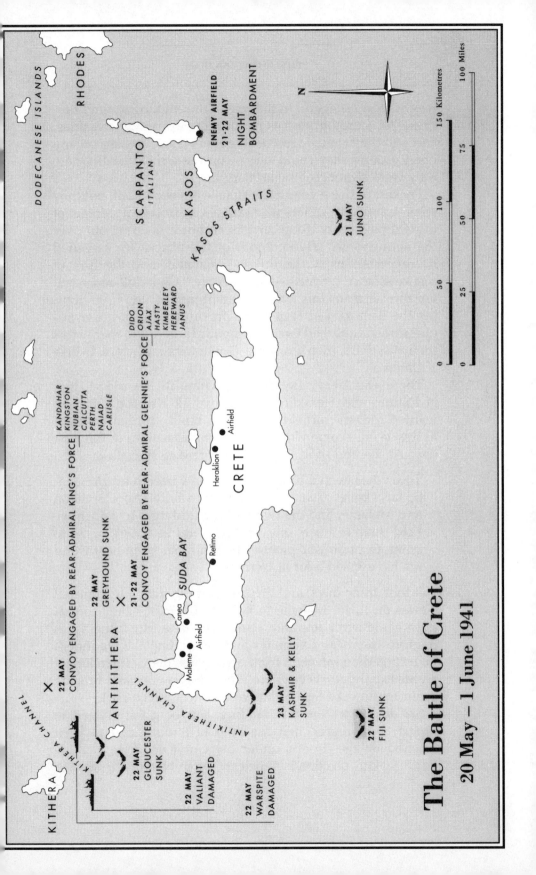

KITHERA

KITHERA CHANNEL

22 MAY
CONVOY ENGAGED BY REAR-ADMIRAL KING'S FORCE

KANDAHAR
KINGSTON
NUBIAN
CALCUTTA
PERTH
NAIAD
CARLISLE

22 MAY
GLOUCESTER
SUNK

22 MAY
VALIANT
DAMAGED

22 MAY
WARSPITE
DAMAGED

ANTIKITHERA

22 MAY
GREYHOUND SUNK

21-22 MAY
CONVOY ENGAGED BY REAR-ADMIRAL GLENNIE'S FORCE

DIDO
ORION
AJAX
HASTY
KIMBERLEY
HEREWARD
JANUS

ANTIKITHERA CHANNEL

Maleme
Airfield
Canea
SUDA BAY
Retimo

CRETE

Heraklion
Airfield

23 MAY
KASHMIR & KELLY
SUNK

22 MAY
FIJI SUNK

DODECANESE ISLANDS

RHODES

SCARPANTO
ITALIAN

ENEMY AIRFIELD
21-22 MAY
NIGHT
BOMBARDMENT

KASOS

KASOS STRAITS

21 MAY
JUNO SUNK

N

0   50   100   150 Kilometres

0   25   50   75   100 Miles

The Battle of Crete
20 May – 1 June 1941

height of its savagery. In the face of unremitting ground fire, these Air Corps troops were suffering appalling casualties, and still they came in, some in gliders crash-landing on any open ground they could see, or on the airfield itself where they were hammered by artillery fire.

Pockets of these young Germans were wiped out, but they were replaced by others who came in an unceasing stream of more than twenty troop-carriers an hour, flooding out over the countryside. 'The strength of the attacks far exceeded the expectations of the British command, and the fury of our resistance astonished the enemy,' Churchill recorded. For the Germans this was a different proposition from fighting the demoralised French the previous year, or the worn-out, under-equipped Greeks a month earlier. The enemy this time was hard men from the Dominions and crack British regiments.

There was heavy fighting elsewhere in the island, too, at Retimo and Heraklion, but above all else the Germans wanted Maleme airfield in order to build up their strength in the days to come without the awful casualties of this first day. At the end of it, Freyberg reported to Wavell:

> Today has been a hard one. We have been hard-pressed. So far, I believe, we hold aerodromes at Retimo, Heraklion and Maleme, and the two harbours. Margin by which we hold them is a bare one, and it would be wrong of me to paint an optimistic picture. Fighting has been heavy and we have killed a lot of Germans.

It took three days, and the loss of more than one hundred planes on it, for Maleme to fall into German hands so that they could with impunity land and take off, bringing in reinforcements and supplies and evacuating the wounded. Like spreading infection from open boils, the German lodgements expanded everywhere. The 5th New Zealand Brigade again fought like tigers, but were slowly forced back.

Six days after the first landing, Freyberg felt obliged to report 'with regret' that the limit of endurance had been reached by the 'troops under my command here at Suda Bay. . . . Our position is hopeless.' As in Norway, it was the incessant bombing and machine-gunning from the air, with no means of reply, that did for them. 'Such continuous and unopposed air attack', Wavell reported to Churchill, 'must drive stoutest troops from positions sooner or later.'

In spite of another form of barrage – exhortations from Churchill that 'victory in Crete essential' – the battle was lost. Relief and salvation could come only from the sea.

11

'I had no illusions about the trickiness of our position'

MOUNTBATTEN AT DAWN, 23 MAY 1941

O n 23 May 1941, four days before the reality of defeat on Crete had to be faced, the Admiralty had signalled Admiral Cunningham with sunny optimism, 'If the Fleet can prevent seaborne reinforcements and supplies reaching the enemy until the Army has had time to deal successfully with all airborne troops, the Army may then be able to deal with seaborne attacks.'

For the testing operations that lay ahead for this hard-pressed fleet, Cunningham himself had decided to work ashore at Alexandria in close liaison with the Army and the RAF. The battle fleet was to be commanded by Vice-Admiral Sir Henry Pridham-Wippell, recently knighted for his work at the Battle of Matapan. Pridham-Wippell had been a destroyer man for most of his service life, commanding the Home Fleet destroyers shortly before the war; immediately before his promotion and knighthood, he had commanded Cunningham's Light Forces.

Under him, Pridham-Wippell was to have Rear-Admirals Glennie and King. Gordon Glennie had only recently arrived in the Mediterranean from commanding HMS *Hood*, which was to suffer the misfortune of being blown up by the *Bismarck* later that month. He could count himself lucky in spite of what lay ahead. Edward King, who arrived

The dreaded Junkers JU 87 Stuka, which nearly did for the carrier *Illustrious* and sank the *Kelly* and many more warships. Against fighters it was hopelessly vulnerable and had to be withdrawn from the Battle of Britain.

HMS *Illustrious* under attack.

The entire company of the *Kelly* photographed at Malta shortly before heading for Crete, where more than half lost their lives.

En route from Malta to Crete on 21 May 1941, the *Kelly* launches a
depth-charge against a suspected submarine and (below) is high-level
bombed by the Italians.

Burning Allied supply ships off Crete.

The *Kelly* capsized and sinking, with survivors on her keel and in the water alongside, photographed from the *Kipling*, which shortly afterwards damaged herself against the *Kelly*'s bows while evading another Stuka attack.

The *Kipling*'s whaler picking up survivors of the *Kelly*, while a sailor in the water seizes a cast line.

Some of the *Kelly*'s survivors in the only carley raft which could be launched before she capsized.

Survivors of the
two destroyers
cram the decks
of the *Kipling* en
route to
Alexandria.

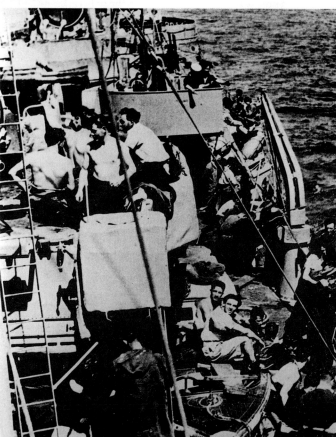

Mountbatten in a borrowed suit goes ashore at Alexandria to be greeted by his nephew, Midshipman Prince Philip, and Admiral Cunningham (centre).

The wounded from the *Kelly* and *Khartoum* being taken off to hospital.

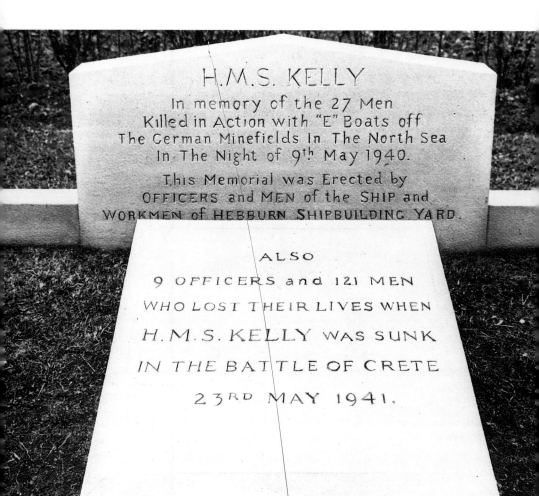

H.M.S. KELLY
In memory of the 27 Men
Killed in Action with "E" Boats off
The German Minefields In The North Sea
In The Night of 9th May 1940.

This Memorial was Erected by
OFFICERS and MEN of the SHIP and
WORKMEN of HEBBURN SHIPBUILDING YARD.

ALSO

9 OFFICERS and 121 MEN

WHO LOST THEIR LIVES WHEN

H.M.S. KELLY WAS SUNK

IN THE BATTLE OF CRETE

23RD MAY 1941.

The Price: it can truly be claimed that the five-week delay to the German attack on the USSR caused by the fighting in Greece and Crete and the eastern Mediterranean changed the course of the Second World War.

to join Cunningham at the same time, was one of those officers sometimes rudely referred to as 'Palace Admirals', having found favour with the Royal Family for one reason or another. He had accompanied the Prince of Wales on his imperial tours after the First World War with Mountbatten and was later appointed Naval ADC to the King.

Intelligence predicted the German airborne attack for the night of 15–16 May, and Cunningham made his dispositions accordingly: Pridham-Wippell with his battleships to the west of Crete to fend off any intervention by the Italian fleet, and light-cruisers and destroyers in three groups south of the island, at night sweeping to the north of Crete for any signs of enemy troop convoys.

The period of five days before the German Air Corps attack had the unfortunate result of reducing uncomfortably the fuel reserves of all Pridham-Wippell's ships. The light craft therefore made a quick dart back to Alexandria to refuel and returned to their patrol lines at once. But Cunningham took the precaution of replacing the battleships, and Rear-Admiral Bernard Rawlings hoisted his flag in the *Warspite* and hastened under destroyer escort to Pridham-Wippell's patrol line west of Crete.

The air assault on the morning of 20 May was witnessed by some of the light forces, and the distant horizon was seen as black with Ju 52 troop-carriers, Ju 88s and Stukas. At dusk, Glennie and King took their five cruisers, two anti-aircraft cruisers and four destroyers, steamed round into the Aegean to search for troop convoys, found nothing and returned to the relative safety of the Mediterranean. But the German command decided that it could spare a few dive-bombers from their work on the island to deal with these warships. They wasted their time – and bombs – unable to press home their attacks against very heavy anti-aircraft fire. This attack was followed, surprisingly, by high-level bombing by Italian Capronis; even more surprisingly, they scored a direct hit on the destroyer *Juno*, the blast penetrating the magazines and blowing up the ship.

On the following day, the RAF succeeded in despatching a long-range aircraft from Egypt to the Aegean. The observer reported clear signs of numerous escorted small ships heading for Suda Bay. Glennie and King set off at once and swept northwards into the Aegean, suffering intense air attack for much of the way. Glennie had the good fortune at around midnight to spot a convoy of packed caiques – he counted twenty-five of them – and several steamers escorted by a single Italian destroyer and several torpedo-boats. His three light-cruisers and four destroyers tore into this mini-armada, guns blazing, switching from target to target with a hail of shells and with vengeful zest for all the bombing they had endured during daylight.

In all, a dozen of these caiques and several of the steamers, as well as an escorting torpedo-boat, were sent to the bottom, killing or drowning some four thousand German troops. Two hours before daylight, Glennie called off his scattered squadron, ordering them to rendezvous west of Crete. They had all expended most of their anti-aircraft ammunition and had no wish to face the wrath of Stukas.

King, to the east and off Heraklion, continued his so-far abortive patrol to the north of the island in daylight, knowing that the heavens must soon open and the bombs fall. Then out of the blue sky came the Junkers, the Stukas almost vertically and the bigger Ju 88s in a steep glide.

His two anti-aircraft cruisers put up a tremendous fire, supplemented by the cruisers' and destroyers' high-angle guns, and by violent evasive manoeuvres succeeded in avoiding every bomb. Soon after the last of these attacks, a single packed caique was sighted and promptly sunk by the Australian cruiser *Perth*. A few minutes later the destroyers dealt with a similarly packed steamer. King pressed on expectantly and the *Perth* next sighted some escort vessels, indicating the proximity of a convoy as large as the one destroyed by Glennie. This was confirmed when one of the escorts began frantically to lay a smoke-screen.

This screen was penetrated by one of King's destroyers, who caught a glimpse of a mass of caiques. Tragically, King's nerve seemed to break at this same moment. In the next hour he could have massacred as many German reinforcements as Glennie had done during the night. Instead, he called off his squadron and turned west for the Kithera Channel. He justified this later by pointing to the slow speed of one of his anti-aircraft cruisers and his low supply of anti-aircraft ammunition.*

It is doubtful if King would have been any more bombed if he had pressed on, which was clearly his duty, than he was as he retreated west to join forces with his fellow squadron. For the next three and a half hours he was under more or less continuous attack from the air. His flagship was badly damaged, with her speed reduced to sixteen knots, and one of his anti-aircraft cruisers was also badly hit and her captain killed on the bridge.

The misfortunes to Rawlings's force continued through the remaining daylight hours. Learning of *Naiad*'s damage and King's shortage of anti-aircraft ammunition, Rawlings steamed east into the Kithera Channel with Glennie's force in support. Within the hour his flagship *Warspite* took a heavy bomb hit, which knocked out all her starboard medium-calibre guns, depriving her of half her anti-aircraft power. Then, shortly after linking up with King's damaged flagship, the destroyer *Greyhound*, which had just sunk a caique, was struck by two bombs and went to the bottom rapidly. Among the survivors was a young ordinary seaman who embarked in the ship's whaler with the destroyer's First Lieutenant and eighteen other seamen. Not satisfied with sinking their ship, one German bomber came down to a low level again and headed for the whaler. This seaman leapt overboard and dived deep in the nick of time. When he resurfaced everyone in the boat had been killed.

Unwisely, King, senior to Rawlings, ordered two more destroyers to pick up survivors, and two cruisers to stand by as well for the benefit of their anti-aircraft power, not realising that they had almost exhausted their ammunition. In any case the Admiral was contravening the basic rule of keeping your force concentrated under air attack.

---

* Cunningham was not pleased. Admiral King was sent home and never served at sea again, retiring before the end of the war.

All these rescue ships were subjected to intense bombing and machine-gunning. King was now reminded by his staff of the near-helplessness of these cruisers and recalled them. However, before they could reach the relative security of Rawlings's big ships, the *Gloucester*, which had survived more bombing over the past months than any other ship, was struck several times. A fire broke out and her upper deck became a shambles of flames and ripped steel before she finally sank.

Her fellow cruiser, *Fiji*, threw carley rafts overboard for any of her surviving company, but almost all of those who had not succumbed already were machine-gunned relentlessly in the water. Her Captain's body was washed up on the other side of the Mediterranean, near Mersa Matruh, a month later.*

However, after she had rejoined the big ships, the *Fiji* lasted only a little longer. A single Me 109, with a 500-pounder under her belly, swept down out of some scattered clouds and dropped her bomb so close that it ripped open the *Fiji*'s bottom. She came to a standstill, listing heavily. In this condition, and with only practice anti-aircraft ammunition left, it was only a matter of time before she was picked off. Soon, a lone Stuka came along, dropped her load of three bombs, and at 8.15 p.m. the *Fiji* rolled over and sank. After dark, two destroyers returned to her grave and picked up 523 of her crew.

So ended this tragic day for the Mediterranean Fleet. The historian Lieutenant-Commander Peter Kemp has written,

> The day had only reinforced the painful lessons learned in Norway and at Dunkirk, that it is not enough to command the seas unless there is command of the air above the sea as well. The air battle had been lost by default before it had begun. . . . Now, because the air battle had been lost, the sea battle and the land battle too were lost and the fate of Crete was sealed.

*　　　*　　　*

* The *Gloucester*'s name is honoured to this day by her near-sister ship, HMS *Belfast*, moored in the Thames at Tower Bridge.

It was most unfortunate that the Admiralty in London appeared to have little appreciation of the realities of what was happening in Cretan waters. To Cunningham's undisguised fury, while one after another of his ships was being blasted by the Luftwaffe, Admiral Pound (with the voice of Churchill ringing through every syllable) repeated 'that the outcome of the battle for Crete would have serious repercussions, and that it was vitally important to prevent seaborne expeditions reaching the island in the next day or two, even if this resulted in further losses to the fleet'.

Cunningham later wrote,

> I replied to this at some length, pointing out that it did not seem to be realised that the withdrawal of all forces to Alexandria had been forced upon me by the necessity for refuelling and because the anti-aircraft ammunition in practically all the ships was spent.

To Cunningham's appreciation that in any case the scale of air attack made it impossible for the Navy to operate in the Aegean or the vicinity of Crete by day, the Chiefs of Staff replied curtly that 'it was essential that the Commanders-in-Chief should concert measures, and that the fleet and the Royal Air Force must accept whatever risk was entailed in preventing any considerable reinforcements from reaching Crete'. It appeared that in London nobody had taken the trouble to use a ruler to calculate the distance of 440 miles from Alexandria to Crete, and discover that there were no fighters capable of reaching the island even if they were available, and that this distance had a bearing on the fuel problems of the fleet, more especially the destroyers.

This 'singularly unhelpful' message was answered by Cunningham:

> It is not the fear of sustaining losses but the need to avoid losses which will cripple the fleet without any commensurate advantage which is the determining factor in operating in the Aegean. . . . The experience of three days in which two cruisers and four destroyers have been sunk, and one battleship, two cruisers and four destroyers damaged,

shows what losses are likely to be. Sea control in the eastern Mediterranean could not be retained after another such experience.

On the morning of 21 May, at the beginning of the Mediterranean Fleet's Crete ordeal, Mountbatten went ashore from the *Kelly*. Valetta was little changed from how they had found it three weeks earlier. The piles of rubbish were a little higher, a few hundred more dwellings had been demolished by the bombing and a number more streets blocked. The same smell of hot dust and putrescence was in the air, like city smog, while above the sky was an intense blue, and the temperature rose with the sun. The dark Maltese people, looking seriously hungry, huddled in their makeshift homes and shelters. The spirit of Malta might be acclaimed in the outside world, but the reality was different.

At naval HQ there were signals from London and Alexandria following the air invasion of Crete on the morning of the previous day. Mountbatten's Flotilla – *Kelly, Kashmir, Kelvin, Kipling* and *Jackal*, all that was left to him – was ordered to 'Rendezvous with C.S.15 (Admiral Rawlings) and C.S.7 (Admiral King) 22 May . . . west of Crete'.

Mountbatten himself sent signals to his Captains and to Beresford to join him at a meeting. Mountbatten explained the situation in the eastern Mediterranean as he understood it and announced the time of departure that evening, 21 May, air-raids permitting. Then they had an informal lunch together. 'It was surprisingly cheerful', Mountbatten recalled, 'considering the circumstances. We were all old friends now and had been through a lot together.'

When he returned to the *Kelly*, he ordered the lower deck cleared. 'I told them that things weren't going too well in the eastern Mediterranean,' he remembered thirty years later, 'that the Germans had carried out a large-scale airborne attack – the biggest in history – on Crete the day before, and that our forces there were hard-pressed. I said, "It's our job to go to support them at once. Make no mistake, things are going to be tough, but we have got to stop any reinforcements from getting through. The chief threat of course will be from the air. But we've faced quite a bit of bombing already, and I trust we're about to increase our score." I ended by saying that I knew they would all live up to my expectations.'

'The Fighting Fifth' steamed out of Valetta harbour, past the ruins on shore and wrecks in the water, for the last time in line ahead, and in the open sea immediately increased speed. There were people on the ramparts waving to them, and they responded cheerfully.

Before darkness fell, they got a 'ping' on the Asdic. The alarm bells rang out and the men were piped to action stations. It was a U-boat, or perhaps an Italian submarine, on the surface, visible from the bridge. But she was crash-diving swiftly and had gone by the time they reached the spot. All four destroyers patterned the area with depth-charges, stirring the peaceful sea into a frenzy of white explosions. Optimistic to the end, Mountbatten thought that they could claim it, but there was no time to follow up the attack or seek evidence. The *Kipling*'s Captain, Commander Aubrey St Clair-Ford, wrote in 1942, 'It seems certain that the submarine was at least damaged.'

It was a sixteen-hour run to Crete, and it was 8 a.m. when the rating up in the rangefinder called down to the bridge. They had been warned that the Italian fleet might come out, and there were big ships on the horizon.

'Ships bearing green 05,' he called.

The bridge thanked him, and he followed up with, 'Rangefinder to bridge. Range 105.'

The bridge thanked him again and reassured him at the same time, 'It's all right, they're ours.'

They were having a hard time, too. In minutes it was possible to identify Rawlings's ships and see the Stukas coming down on to them. They were on the scene exactly as the *Warspite* took a heavy hit on her starboard side, dust and debris rising high above the flagship. All around the white spouts of exploding bombs rose as high as the battleship's foremast. She looked now as she had looked at the Battle of Jutland twenty-five years earlier – '*Warspite*, apparently stopped in a forest of water spouts, doomed as it seemed to destruction, but replying to the enemy fire with all her guns,' as the official historian of the battle wrote. 'A real game old lady,' was the common view.

'Now it was our turn,' Mountbatten recounted. 'Some of the bombers had spotted us and seemed to fancy this new target.' They were twin-engine Ju 88s, around half a dozen, and they chose to run up at high level, which was a relief. For a while the destroyers' 4.7s could fire, but almost at once they were beyond their elevation capacity and too high for their light anti-aircraft guns, leaving only the single four-inchers to keep up the fire. One stick of bombs pursued the *Kelly* from astern, the splashes advancing at the speed of the bomber, the last evaded only by a quick turn of the helm.

When the bombing was over, Mountbatten closed the flagship for instructions from Rawlings: 'Search for survivors from *Gloucester* and *Fiji*.' Learning that the *Kingston* was near the stricken ship, he asked the destroyer to transmit its call-sign so that DF (direction-finding) bearings could be obtained. They reached the positions in less than half an hour, but there was nothing to be seen – no *Kingston*, no ships at all, no wreckage, no survivors: just a smooth, empty sea and a clear dusk sky as if peace had unexpectedly come.

It was a brief peace, a few minutes only, then the signals office picked up an appeal from General Freyberg to Admiral Rawlings: 'Naval bombardment of Maleme aerodrome would be appreciated.' The time of origin was 18.56.

Rawlings at once signalled to 'Captain (D) 5', ordering him to comply. 'So *Kelly*, *Kashmir* and *Kipling* altered course to the westward', ran St Clair-Ford's report, 'and proceeded at high speed to our patrol area. When in the Antikitheron Channel, *Kipling* developed steering trouble and every effort was made to have it repaired as soon as possible.' Meanwhile, Mountbatten with *Kelly* and *Kashmir* raced for Maleme to carry out his new mission. On the way, the radar picked up two blips, which were no more than a mile away.

Mountbatten ordered 'Open shutters!' and the *Kelly*'s and *Kashmir*'s searchlights picked out two caiques, loaded to the gunwales with German troops, packs on their backs ready to land. The two destroyers opened fire with their 4.7s, the shells tearing the vulnerable boats – and their passengers – apart. A third caique was also spotted. It must have been loaded with fuel for it blew up with a mighty flash and disappeared. They could hear the cries of the helpless Germans in the sea as they continued on their way and closed to within two thousand yards from the shore.

The bombardment of the airfield lasted only a few minutes, but it seemed to have been effective and certainly improved the spirits of the hard-pressed Australian and New Zealanders. 'We cheered like hell', one later reported, 'when we saw the gun flashes from seaward and when the shells landed right on target and none landed in our own lines.'

A tragic and unforgiveable signalling error was to help seal the fate of Mountbatten's ship. While the *Kelly* was employing her guns to such effect in the night (22–23 May), Cunningham was checking on the ammunition supply of Rawlings's big ships. The reply was alarming. It seemed, according to the hand-written signal, that they were empty of short-range ammunition. The following morning the typed confirmation came through, which read that, on the contrary, they had 'plenty' of ammunition. It was too late. During the night the signal had been sent out that all ships should return to Alexandria, the reason being that without the support of the *Valiant* and the *Warspite*, the risk for the smaller ships, and especially the destroyers, was too great.

The *Kipling* was some six miles distant from the *Kashmir* and the *Kelly*, after the fault to her steering had been diagnosed and repaired. 'We followed up the Fleet at our best speed,' reported the *Kipling*'s Captain 'and by dawn we were unpleasantly close to the south-west corner of Crete, doing all we knew to leave that unhealthy area.'

They could no longer depend on the protection of the battleships and dawn light was already setting aglow the eastern horizon. If ever there was a time for full speed it was now, and the *Kelly*'s motto 'Keep On' was never more closely adhered to. From her the only ships in sight were the distant *Kipling* and the *Kashmir* one mile away. Every gun was manned, every man keyed up.

On the pom-pom they could not remember how long they had been closed up at the gun. The gun captain looked at his crew, dirty, eyes red-rimmed, unshaven and desperately tired, and thought, 'Blimey, do I look like that, too?' [wrote Kenneth Poolman]

'Dusty' Dunsterville had been approached by Chief Petty Officer Primrose. 'Sir, my [signal] lads are all in. Can't we pack up on two frequencies? – they've been up all night.'

Mountbatten was as tired as any of them. 'I remembered that it was my father's birthday tomorrow. I always remembered it, and always thought of him when the going was rough,' he recalled. 'I had no illusions about the trickiness of our position. We could expect no support from any other ships, and certainly not from the air. We would certainly have been reported by the Germans round Maleme, and it could be only a matter of time before we were picked up.'

A single aircraft had been spotted distantly at 6 a.m. It was as inevitable as this day had followed night that there would soon be more than one aircraft hovering in the sky.

Just as Primrose was making his appeal, an internal signal came in: 'Radar bridge, radar bridge. Large formation of aircraft approaching from astern.' Their ordeal was minutes away.

12

Fame Too Soon?

T he sequence of events that followed this sighting was so swift and violent that accounts vary and the narrative sometimes becomes as blurred as the impression left in the memories of the survivors. Some eye-witnesses were emphatic about certain scenes, none more so than Mountbatten himself. Others began, 'As far as I can remember, but it was a long time ago. . . .'

What is not disputed is that it was 8 a.m., 23 May 1941; it was already hot, the sun was well up and there were twenty-four Stukas approaching from the north over Crete in eight tight-bunched groups of stacked 'vics' of three. Nor did anyone dispute that at about eight thousand feet, when they were overhead, these Stukas turned on their backs and came down in their usual breathtakingly steep dives, splitting up to divide the defensive fire, sirens screaming defiance.

St Clair-Ford, on the bridge of the repaired *Kipling* six miles distant, and about ten miles from the Crete coastline beyond, wrote soon after the events of this day:

HA [high-angle] gunfire was observed between us and the coast between 0630 and 0700, but we could not see who was firing. About 0740, *Kelly* and *Kashmir* were sighted to the northwards and V/S [visual signalling] communication was established. I altered course to close them slightly but at 0800 we were shattered to see a swarm of about twenty to thirty dive-bombers carrying out a concentrated attack on these ships. The first waves were avoided by both ships. . . .

The *Kelly* was at thirty knots, cleared for action as she had been since the previous day, the gun crews, ears muffled against blast, closed up, the four-inch HA already in action, the gun making that characteristic cracking sound that threatened the most protected eardrums. Then there was Lieutenant Hutchinson with Rocky Wilkins and the rest of the team on the pom-pom platform, Ted West with his twin Oerlikons, and the rest with the multiple .5s and Lewis .303s.

The 4.7s were closed up, too, the gun crews hunched behind the flash shields in case they had an opportunity to open fire. Never had the criminal folly of restricting the elevation of these big guns to forty degrees been more starkly exemplified. With high-angle facility, the two destroyers could have been staining the sky and demoralising the German aircrews with heavy shellfire before entering their dive, twelve guns firing fifteen rounds a minute or better, instead of their single four-inch.

Some reports said that there were two attacks which were foiled before the fatal one on both the *Kashmir* and the *Kelly*. St Clair-Ford thought that they were caught in the second one. Others, like Dunsterville, said, 'A single Stuka came straight down on us, down to less than four hundred feet I'd say. It couldn't miss. I never saw any earlier attacks that some people mention, just one bomb on the *Kashmir* and one on us. And that was it.'

Possibly the first Stuka dropped the fatal bomb – it was always easier being first – and others followed. Certainly Ted West at the lethal Oerlikons got one. According to one of his mates, 'A third of the way through its dive he opened fire and I saw his tracers going right home and pieces breaking off the bomber, which burst into bright flames and crashed into the sea.'

Others thought that they saw parachutes, but this was very unlikely: there would not have been time to get out. Many, including Mountbatten and Dunsterville on the bridge, saw the fatal bomb coming straight at them and they both knew that it could not miss.

'It was just like that torpedo a year earlier, except that this time I knew we weren't going to survive,' Mountbatten remembered. 'It hit square on X gundeck, killing the 4.7 crew instantly, and exploded just abaft the engine-room. I gave the order "Midships" when the sound of the explosion had died, and then "Hard a-port". But it was no good, and we listed over more heavily than ever.' It was like willing a dead man back to life. The Coxswain shouted up the voice-pipe, 'Ship won't answer the helm, sir. No reply from the engine-room telegraphs.'

Although, for once, they were right to be doing thirty knots, it did result in the water tearing in like a tidal wave, drowning or smashing many men below decks.

Oddly, in the midst of this horror and tumult, a number of the crew had time to see the *Kashmir* being hit at almost the same time. Again, some said she capsized at once, others that she broke in two, others again that she floated long enough to launch five carley rafts. St Clair-Ford reported that the *Kashmir* received one or two hits amidships and that she broke her back and sank within two minutes. Who could ever tell for sure in this nightmarish turmoil?

Mountbatten was shouting 'Keep firing!', but no one heard him; those who were still alive were doing so anyway. Beresford was at the four-inch, which was firing flat out, the crew co-ordinating with the precision of a machine until the swivel jammed with empty shell cases. Like a manic housemaid, someone seized a broom and tried to sweep them away.

One able seaman, escaping from the damaged section of the ship, suddenly turned and saw that he was being followed by 'a file of burnt and blackened scarecrows', the leader scorched from head to foot, his ears burnt clear away. It was just one of the surreal and momentary images that many of the survivors retained.

On the bridge Mountbatten and Dunsterville, in tin helmets, remained completely calm, holding on against the angle of the ship. Mountbatten wrote later to his elder daughter, 'I felt I ought to be the last to leave the ship and I left it a bit late because the bridge turned over on top of me and I was trapped in the boiling, seething cauldron underneath.'

Mountbatten told this writer, 'I was clutching the gyro pedestal on the bridge. We were over beyond ninety degrees, and then the sea came in a roaring maelstrom. I saw officers and men struggling to get out of the bridge, then I took an enormously deep breath as the water closed over my head.

'I felt the pressure on my lungs and kept one hand over my mouth and the other over my nose. I came up in the end, but it seemed an awfully long time. The first thing I saw was the stern of the ship no more than a dozen yards away, travelling fast, propellers still rotating. Butler-Bowdon was near me and I shouted at him "Swim like hell!" A nasty end being chewed up. The ship just missed us, still travelling fast.

'When I paused for breath and looked around, an oil-stained head popped up beside me. It was a stoker petty officer, and he said at once, "Funny how the scum always comes to the top, sir!"'

Sidney Mosses remembered the speed with which things happened between sighting the bombers and hitting the water. 'The ship was twisting and turning, the noise of the guns, the smoke, turning hard to starboard when I saw that the ship's side was folded up like a sardine tin, right up to the pom-pom, over and over she went, thought this is it, and over we went still going at full speed, remember seeing the funnel go into the sea. . . .'

Dunsterville, officer of the watch at the time, remembers 'just clinging on for as long as I could – then I was swept down, came up too near the propellers for comfort and went down again. When I resurfaced I seemed to have "Rocky" Wilkins on my back, holding on to my big American lifebelt. There were a lot of us bobbing about and we found bits of wood to hold on to. The water was very warm, but the oil was awful. It got into your stomach and mouth and gummed up your eyes.'

Someone had managed to cut loose a single carley raft, which saved a number of lives. Mountbatten was calling out, 'Swim to the raft!'

Nowhere in the ship was the fight for life grimmer and more tenacious than down in the engine-room. Many were dead or hopelessly trapped, but there were some who escaped. When Commander Evans knew the Stukas were about to attack, he hurried below and spoke to the Chief Engine-Room Artificer.

'Stand by for squalls,' he warned. 'There's a host of aircraft coming up astern.'

The message was passed from man to man without much fuss. Someone said, 'Go and get a cricket bat and bash off the bombs, then.' It was not very funny, but it caused local laughter.

A moment after that the ship shook like a wet terrier. At first Evans thought it was a near miss, then the deck began to tilt under him and all the lights went out. The secondary lighting, a mere glow, came on and the Engineer Officer could see the faces of the men about him and was reassured as he reached to answer the telephone. There was only noise, like a train in a tunnel, and he put it back on its hook, but with difficulty for the ship was lurching violently to port.

They were all on the deck, and Evans told them to get up. Their tools, torn from their hooks, had become lethal missiles instead of vital accessories to their trade. The secondary lighting flickered out as the oil spilt, then caught fire on the deck and bulkhead, giving them bright light for a few seconds before the flame spluttered and died.

The water was coming in quite fast through a square hatch in the centre of the engine-room and was soon up to their knees. Then Evans was splashed in the face by water, a reminder that their situation was desperate. A second later the *Kelly* was upside down and someone was calling, 'Where's that bloody hatch?'

The speed of the capsizing meant that the air in the engine-room had been trapped, 'forming an air-lock so that the sea had flooded the compartment to a depth of only about four feet above what was originally the upper deck but which was now the bottom,' ran one account of their situation. 'The pale green disc that they saw was the light shining through the circular hatch and the few feet of water above it . . .

One of the men reached up, grabbed the hatch rim and pulled himself up feet first. He felt like a big man trying to get into a small attic trap in his house. But he got through and then swam horizontally with the ship above him until he became entangled in the guardrails and the davits of the motor cutter. The boat would have been useful if he could have released it, but that was mere fantasy and anyway his lungs were bursting. He dragged himself free and shot to the surface, to the blinding light and the oil and the dimly seen bobbing heads about him. The Engine-Room Artificer surfaced beside him, gasping, spitting and crying out, and several more followed.

Commander Evans had remained for a second and had shouted, 'Is anybody else here?' There was only an echo in the strange silence. He threw off his tin helmet and followed the others through the hatch. He, too, struck some part of the deck fittings before he kicked himself free and found himself close to the capsized *Kelly*'s side; too close, and he called out to the others near him to get clear or they would be sucked down.

Evans looked back when he was far enough away and saw the whole length of the inverted ship, still moving slowly through the water, propellers lazily turning, two or three men clinging on to her keel. Beresford, Dunsterville and then Mountbatten himself were seen dragging exhausted or wounded men to the raft, where they were pulled aboard by those already inside.

Rocky Wilkins had detached himself from Dunsterville's big American lifebelt and had found an empty beer crate, which gave him just enough buoyancy. Like Ted West at the Oerlikons, he had been dragged from his seat while his eye was still at the gunsight.

Mountbatten threw away his tin helmet – not suitable for

swimming – but regretted it at once when the Stukas came down again and began machine-gunning, or so he maintained. Others claim they were not interfered with. 'I don't remember any machine-gunning,' Dunsterville recalled; nor did Lieutenant Peter Ashmore in the comparative safety of the *Kipling*'s bridge. But Mountbatten insisted that he helped some wounded on to the carley raft and recalled the wretched necessity of dragging out the machine-gunned dead.

The fact that they were all half- or wholly blind, and half-deaf, too, from the effects of the oil added to the confusion and contradiction of impressions. Those who died might have been mortally wounded earlier, and the shock element also has to be taken into account. At least, unlike the Atlantic in winter, you did not die from the combined cold and shock within minutes.

Mountbatten continued his narrative: 'The sea was beautifully warm and calm – just the sort of sea people look forward to when they go to the Mediterranean for a holiday. But now we all needed cheering up and I called for a song or two. We began with "Roll out the barrel". The *Kelly* wasn't far off, bottom up, but she was going, so I called out "Three cheers for the old ship". . . .'

It was 'Bless our Ship' all over again, even if there were only seconds of life left to her, and with all those trapped inside, and those already dead, the prayer carried with it a last message of pity and lamentation from shipmates freed to shipmates doomed.

She went down quite quickly after this, but not deep and with her stem sticking out like the nose of a drowning man. There was none of the 'suck' of most sinking ships and those on the keel just swam away. The *Kelly* was holding on as if reluctant to commit herself to the deep, or perhaps she had more mischief in mind?

The *Kipling* had been too far distant for the Stukas to spot her in the frenzy of the attack on the *Kashmir* and the *Kelly*. It had been most fortunate that the destroyer had been delayed for she would certainly have been attacked and sunk, too. St Clair-Ford reported:

We immediately closed the position to rescue survivors. On our arrival at the scene, some of the Stukas were flying around and maching-gunning survivors in the water but they cleared off on our arrival, with the exception of one.

I stopped close to the upturned *Kelly*, whose stem was just showing above the water when this remaining Stuka delivered a dive-bombing attack on *Kipling*. I went full ahead under rudder but, my attention being fully taken up with this attacking Stuka, I went too close to *Kelly*'s stem which passed down my starboard side just after the Stuka's attack was delivered, the bomb falling about twenty yards off my port side. The result of this collision with the wreckage of the *Kelly* caused the ship's side to be opened up for'd, resulting in loss of stability and a list of about six degrees to starboard, and causing *Kipling* to be about six feet down by the bow.

There were worse consequences, impossible to anticipate but sufficient to prove the *Kelly*'s proneness to mishap even in her death throes.

Peter Ashmore remembers that single Stuka, too. He was giving orders to the wheelhouse, guiding the *Kipling* to the groups of survivors. 'We had picked up one or two of the biggest clusters. The *Kelly* was upside down on our starboard bow across our path, stem sticking out, and we did not see her early enough. Then this Stuka came at us and all eyes were on it. The collision gouged a hole in the feed tank, and we just avoided by an inch or two having to flood the pom-pom magazine.'

Almost all the *Kashmir*'s survivors were in the five carley rafts, and it was the *Kelly*'s men who were in more urgent need of rescue. Some were able to swim to the nets and drag themselves on-board; others could just make it but had to be helped up, hands greasy with oil, to collapse on the deck. The carley raft with its wounded posed the biggest problem, and it took nearly two hours to get these men on-board, one or two expiring on the way.

The *Kipling*'s men were like male nurses, washing oil from

mouths and eyes, and from wounds, their one medicine being a stiff whisky. That went down all right. The doctor and his mate gave injections of morphia where required and ordered some of the men to the sick-bay.

At last attention could be given to the *Kashmir*'s survivors a mile away, and the procedure started all over again. It was while the first of these men were being helped on-board that the sound of bombers was again heard, a distant, deep thunder of doom; high up in the blue sky a formation of twin-engine Heinkels could be made out.

'This was the first of 108 bomber attacks on the *Kipling*,' Dunsterville said recently. 'Yes, 108. I counted them, every one, and how we evaded them all I've no idea.' (St Clair-Ford made it ninety-eight.)

'With great skill and courage', Mountbatten recalled, 'Commander St Clair-Ford nosed his way from one raft to another in between the persistent air attacks.'

St Clair-Ford's own report ran:

> We then moved across to *Kashmir*'s survivors about a mile away, but rescue work was considerably delayed owing to a series of high-level bombing attacks carried out one by one, two or three aircraft at a time. It would have been too hazardous to remain stopped whilst these attacks were in progress and so, as soon as one was seen to be commencing *Kipling* got under way so as to be able to dodge the bombs and also with the object of getting away from the survivors to avoid them being injured by near misses in their vicinity. So, as can be seen, rescue work was slow and an extremely anxious undertaking. . . .

Water spouts rose from the sea on all sides, and the pom-poms rattled away, the .5s joining in when they were low enough, the single four-inch when they were higher. These twin-engine planes bombed either from a high level or came in in a shallow glide which lacked the deadly accuracy of the Stukas. But as noon came and went it seemed that only intervention from the highest authority could have led to every bomb, from 50 to 500 kg., missing the ship.

No sooner had she picked up more of the *Kashmir*'s survivors than another bombing attack developed and the *Kipling* had to make off at full speed, limited now to about twenty-two knots, for further evasive evolutions, like some ballet *entr'acte*.

St Clair-Ford, reckoning that they would never finish the job at this rate, ordered the *Kipling*'s fast motor-boat to be lowered during a lull, with the intention that she should pick up as many survivors as she could and transfer them to the destroyer when opportunity offered.

A party of men got the big boat into the water with great speed and efficiency, but there was no quick-release gear and the falls had to be unshackled by hand. Before this could be done St Clair-Ford yelled, 'Bomber approaching, am going full ahead.' Mountbatten repeated the message and added urgently, 'Cut the falls!'

Knives flashed, and in this emergency someone cut the foremost falls first, which was highly dangerous under the circumstances. As the *Kipling* accelerated the bows of the motor-boat turned out sharply and she began to capsize.

Mountbatten yelled, 'You bloody fools, cut the after falls!'

They were too late. The 40,000-horsepower engines of the *Kipling* were thrusting her through the sea. St Clair-Ford recorded:

> This caused the motor-boat to be towed stern first for a time, but unfortunately the fall did not part, neither was the stern ring bolt of the motor-boat pulled out. Both davits were pulled down and I regret to have to record that although I did not know about this until about an hour afterwards, they took with them my First Lieutenant (Lieutenant-Commander John Bush) and the First Lieutenant of the *Kelly* (Lieutenant-Commander Lord Hugh Beresford).

Mountbatten's own account did not fundamentally differ. 'Together Beresford and Bush leaped to the after falls at the moment when the ship had gathered such speed and the heavy motor-boat had sunk so deep in the water that the after davit was pulled right over and seemed to crush them as the falls tore away and the boat sank in the sea together with the two First Lieutenants.'

Once more the *Kipling* avoided another flurry of bombs and turned back as the bombers headed for home. They were given ten clear minutes to collect another dozen survivors with the whaler. It was at about this time that a somewhat hectic discussion took place on the *Kipling*'s bridge. Its subject, between alarms, was the delicate balance of risk between steaming clear of this lethal area and heading for Egypt with the two hundred or so men they already had on-board, or continuing with this highly dangerous darting clear to avoid the bombs and returning to pick up the men still in the water or carley rafts.

Lieutenant Harry Kidston* of the *Kipling* favoured launching all the destroyer's remaining boats and carley rafts, including the powered dinghy, leaving the survivors to head for the coast, which was little more than three miles distant. This would have possibly been acceptable if they had not lost the big motor-boat which could have towed the carley rafts and the whaler, but the little dinghy was quite inadequate for the task.

Mountbatten and St Clair-Ford favoured the humanitarian but risky course of picking up the remainder as rapidly as possible, and this they did, or so they thought, in a temporary and merciful lull. Satisfied that there was no one left, St Clair-Ford called for full speed and they steamed south from this melancholy scene where so many of their shipmates had died, trailing a highly visible line of leaking oil. It was not until later that Mountbatten learned that a single figure was seen to rise from the abandoned whaler and salute their departure. Perhaps he succeeded in rowing to the land. No one ever knew.

They were bombed intermittently almost until dusk, mainly by single Heinkel He 111s from a height beyond the range of the pom-poms and where only the single four-inch could reach them. In view of their loss of oil St Clair-Ford requested a ship from Alexandria to top up their tanks at dawn.

---

* Brother of the South African motor-racing ace, Glen Kidston.

By midnight Mountbatten knew that they were not going to make it to port without a supplementary supply of fuel, and without it their ability to evade further bombing was nil. As the sun rose, equally anxious eyes scanned the northern horizon for signs of renewed bombing and the southern horizon for the funnel smoke of the ship that could relieve the tense anxiety which they had experienced without relief for twenty-four hours.

The *Kipling* was down to a few tons of fuel when the well-named guardship *Protector* hove into sight ahead. She got a great cheer when she came alongside and a line was cast between the two ships, which were then linked by the *Protector*'s hose. St Clair-Ford took on fifteen tons, just enough to get them safely to port.

By mid-morning the low skyline of Egypt could be seen ahead, and then individual palm trees and white buildings shimmering in the heat. St Clair-Ford addressed the greatly enlarged ship's company through a loudhailer, his own men and the three hundred or so black-stained survivors from the *Kelly* and the *Kashmir* ranged about the upper deck of his ship like victims of a holocaust. He told them:

> The Fleet has heard of your magnificent action and all the trials you have undergone. They are waiting there in Alexandria to welcome you into the harbour. As we go through the boom gates they will be assembled on the upper decks of their ships, waiting to give you a rousing welcome.

The Mediterranean Fleet, missing many fine ships and others showing the damage of battle, had only recently returned from Cretan waters – the great battleships, the cruisers and destroyers, the carrier *Formidable*, whose fighters, if she had had any, might have saved them. The reception, the cheers and waving caps from every ship, was indeed tremendous. It began before they entered the gates and continued until they secured alongside No. 46 pier. Those on-board the *Kipling* who could stand were at the rails, a solid phalanx of oil-stained, oddly dressed, dead-weary sailors, waving in answer to the accolades: a moving sight which brought tears to the eyes of many who witnessed the scene.

There were ambulances and trucks and coaches on the quayside. The men with stretchers were first on-board, tenderly collecting the worst wounded and taking them away.

The spirit of Rudyard Kipling seemed to blend with the occasion and the ship named after the poet, who had written forty-three years earlier in the last lines of his poem 'Destroyers':

> Good luck to those that see the end,
> Goodbye to those that drown –
> For each his chance as chance shall send –
> And God for all! *Shut down!*

Dunsterville recalled, 'I seem to remember quite a reception, but I don't remember much – we were all so tired – completely flaked out. Mountbatten had lost his Secretary and he co-opted me instead, so we went together to stay with Admiral Cunningham, whom I knew privately anyway. The first thing was a nice hot bath!'

Mountbatten, in a civilian suit someone had dug up for him, strode down the gangway the moment it was in position, Dunsterville following him. There was, surprisingly, a tall, fair-haired midshipman waiting to greet them, standing beside Cunningham. Mountbatten recognised his nephew, Prince Philip, who was serving in the battleship *Valiant* and was roaring with laughter.

'I didn't think that there was much to laugh at and asked him what was up. "You've no idea how funny you look," Philip said. "You look like a nigger minstrel." I realised then how smothered with oil I still was.'

All four, including Dunsterville, got into a car and were driven to Cunningham's quarters, where Mountbatten cabled Edwina in London: 'Once again all right but this time heartbroken.'

The men were taken to the supply ship *Resource*, where they had a bath and a meal and were issued with cigarettes and chocolate. Then they returned to No. 46 gate and in the shed were given an assortment of clothes from stores that were inadequate for their needs: pith helmets instead of caps for instance, which made them look like a gathering of colonial officers, and white tropical shoes and officers' fancy underclothes. They thought all this very funny. Their resilience was remarkable, and although there was grief for lost shipmates – 121 of them from the *Kelly* alone as well as nine officers – the relief and elation of improbable survival could not be entirely suppressed.

Tents had been set up for them at the Fleet Air Arm station at Dhekeila, and there they settled down for their first night's peaceful sleep since they had arrived at Malta nearly four weeks earlier. They saw Mountbatten for the last time when he visited them. He was looking spruce in borrowed tropical white uniform, his two rows of medals and immaculate white cap. He was full of enthusiasm, as if he had won a famous victory instead of losing his ship and so many of his officers and men. He talked to the men individually, assuring them that wives and mothers had learned already that they were safe. 'Now you'll be able to marry your Doris when you get home,' he might say to one, or 'I hope you hear better news of your mother, Charlie.' His touch with the lower deck was, as always, just right, and it made them feel that there was nothing shaming about losing their ship.

Then he climbed on to a handy wooden crate and spoke to them all:

I have come to say goodbye to the few of you who are left [he began]. We have had so many talks, but this is our last. I have always tried to crack a joke or two before and you have all been friendly and laughed at them. But today I'm afraid I have run out of jokes, and I don't suppose any of us feel much like laughing. The *Kelly* has been in one scrap after another, but even when we have had men killed the majority survived and brought the old ship back. Now she lies in 1,500 fathoms and with her more than half our shipmates. If they had to die, what a grand way to go, for now they all lie together with the ship we loved, and they are in very good company. We have lost her, but they are still with her. There may be less than half the *Kelly* left, but I feel that each of us has twice as good a reason to fight.

You will be sent to replace men who have been killed in other ships, and the next time you are in action remember the *Kelly*. As you ram each shell home into the gun, shout, *Kelly*! and so her spirit will go on inspiring us until victory is won.

I should like to add that there isn't one of you I wouldn't be proud and honoured to serve with again. Goodbye, good luck, and thank you all from the bottom of my heart.

No naval commander could have improved on, nor even matched, that for a farewell speech to his men. If volunteers had been called for to return to those bomber-infested waters around Crete, there would have been no difficulty in forming a ship's company under this man. Mountbatten was the very personification of leadership, and that is the single, simple reason why he inspired his men, at sea or later in the jungles of Burma, to give their utmost, and then a little more. As a destroyer captain in peace they were prepared to make that final effort – just a little more than any other competitors – which had brought to an earlier ship's company the award 'Cock of the Fleet'.

Among themselves, there was never a breath of criticism on the *Kelly*'s mess decks. It would have been considered dishonourable anyway, such was their pride at having gone through so many dangers with him, and survived. When, later, unfavourable comments were heard, the men who had served under him were outraged. It was like being told that your father had a criminal record, and they reacted strongly. It was put down to jealousy, jealousy of his royal rank, his ebullient style, his success and his promotion to dizzy heights. His responsibilities and achievements all seemed to support their estimate of their one-time leader.

It is true that his superior officers were often affronted by his cheerful informality, his constant chatter and breathtaking egotism. His overwhelming need to 'make a splash' on every occasion offended many fellow officers, just as it was regarded with proprietorial pride by the lower deck. They were thrilled at the way he brought the *Kelly* into harbour at a higher speed than any other captain would dare to attempt, proud of the way they were always in the van.

John Coote, now a respected retired Captain RN, and in 1940 'duty doggie' to Captain William Tennant commanding the battle-cruiser *Repulse*, recalls a morning at Scapa Flow:

As the bugler sounded 'carry on' after Colours had been hoisted, the officer of the watch called: '*Kelly* entering harbour, sir. Saluting us to port.' Bill Tennant moved to the port ladder as *Kelly* swept through the lines of anchored battleships, aircraft carriers and cruisers, heading for the destroyer berths. She looked magnificent, with the pendants streaming from her halyards, everything properly squared away, with her flamboyant CO prominently saluting as his piping party of four (more usual to have only two in wartime) sounded off. She was making twenty-five knots at the time. Her wash bashed all our boats against our armoured belt, doing some damage. As Tennant turned away from the little ceremonial, he remarked quietly, 'Captain Mountbatten is, I am sure, a very gallant officer. But as a practical seaman I have my doubts.'

Captain Coote also noted, even at his young age, that Mountbatten had deliberately chosen 0900 hours as his time of arrival so as to be the focus of attention of every flag and commanding officer in the Home Fleet. 'An hour earlier it would have been dark.'

You could react to scenes like this in two ways: you could deplore them for being arrogant and in bad taste, a poor example to junior officers. 'His vanity, though child-like,' Philip Ziegler has written, 'was monstrous.' Or you could indulgently class them as a harmless piece of showing off by a man well endowed with so many qualities that it was impossible not to forgive him. The second judgment was that of his countless admirers, and not all from the lower deck, and his multitude of relations and personal friends who loved him.

This rather tiresome showing off certainly never told against the standing in which he was held by Churchill, the man most responsible for his subsequent meteor-like rise in rank and responsibility. But then one has to add the rider that Churchill's judgment of character was not infallible.

Within the context of the *Kelly* and Mountbatten's leadership of the 5th Flotilla, there can be no doubt that he was admired by officers and men. Captain Dunsterville, who was closer to him than any other officer from his appointment as signals officer in June 1938 until Mountbatten's departure from Egypt in late May 1941, today summarises his belief in these words: 'The sailors really loved him and thought the world of him. I think all the officers held him in great affection. I absolutely adored him as a person. He got the very best out of everyone – the men, the officers and his Staff. It was a very happy ship. Somehow we didn't take much regard of the many clangers. They were just part of war. It was only when it was all over that we began to think about the clangers.'

'I like and admire Mountbatten,' Cunningham once told Dudley Pound, but when offered Mountbatten or the future Admiral Sir John Edelsten, who was nine years older, as his Chief of Staff, Cunningham reckoned Edelsten to be the sounder of the two and chose him. In the heat of crisis, he also noted to another officer who had survived the *Kelly*'s sinking, 'The trouble with your flotilla, boy, is that it was thoroughly badly led.'

Mountbatten's official biographer reached a similar reluctant conclusion that he was not a good flotilla leader, for all his leadership qualities, nor even a good wartime commander of destroyers. Mountbatten's choice of the *Kelly*'s motto 'Keep On' does not tell all, but adhered to as it was it is a guide to the reasons for Mountbatten's failure, and certainly for the 'clangers' in the North Sea, the Channel, off Brest and Benghazi, and the knife-edge escape off Namsos.

Mountbatten liked records, and breaking them. He would

time his drives from his home in London to the dockyard at Portsmouth, and was thrilled to bits when he knocked off a minute or two. The black rubber marks on the A3 road testified to the number of near shaves. Apart from the risk of killing a few people, and himself, this could be counted as youthful fun, though actually it went on into middle age and beyond. When it came to chasing German destroyers, with the resulting terrible loss of life, or failing to secure the release of 600 incarcerated sailors in the case of the *City of Flint*, it is necessary to take a more severe view. To quote his biographer again:

> He pushed his ship fast for little reason except his love of speed and imposed unnecessary strain on his own officers and the other ships in the flotilla. He allowed himself to be distracted from his main purpose by the lure of attractive adventures. Above all he lacked that mysterious quality of 'sea sense', the ability to ensure that one's ship is in the right place at the right time.

The same applied to his driving and flying: his love of the sensational came before the more humdrum need to relate to the machine.

There are so many but mostly intangible merits to set against all these true but sad judgments. His optimism, his exuberance, his style and ability to get the best out of people are all the least quantifiable. More assessable from 1936 was his important endeavour to alert and prepare the Royal Navy for the impact of air-power on the Fleet, and it is ironical that his success was rewarded by the loss of his own ship by air bombardment. He had seen what a few modern fighters could do against bombing attack when he was towing home the wreck of the *Javelin*; but they got him when there was not an Allied fighter within four hundred miles.

To the general public, the wartime figure of Mountbatten, the one-time darling of the socialites and gossip writers, was the personification of heroism; his splendid looks, tall upright figure, two rows of medals, gold-braided cap at a slight tilt, striding along to the Admiralty, was a sight to lift the hearts of a bombed, blacked-out people. Never mind that HMS *Kelly*'s career was so short and made briefer by a series of mishaps; never mind that this fine destroyer did not contribute very much directly to the war effort; when linked with the name Lord Louis Mountbatten in the processes of war propaganda, much encouraged by Mountbatten himself, she provided a great boost to morale.

Until March 1941, the RAF with its triumphant record in the Battle of Britain, the only great pivotal battle to be witnessed by half the nation, had attracted the greatest acclaim among the three services. Now it was the Navy's turn. The triumph at Taranto in the winter, followed by the Battle of Matapan, the rescues of Allied armies by the Mediterranean Fleet from Greece and Crete, culminating in 'the gallant fight of Lord Mountbatten's *Kelly*', and the destruction of the mighty *Bismarck*, brought great acclaim to the Royal Navy.

When Noël Coward, wearing Mountbatten's cap, but for modesty's sake under another name, played him in the film *In Which We Serve*, the myth became firmly established everywhere, and HMS *Kelly* became the most renowned rather than the most needlessly battered ship of the war.

Meanwhile, within a couple of days of his arrival at Alexandria, Mountbatten was off in a determined mood to Middle East Command HQ in Cairo and to the Embassy. There he made clear, in very strong language, what he thought of the RAF's 'total neglect of its responsibilities' during the battle for Crete. This was hardly the RAF's immediate fault for there were no long-range fighters available, and the one carrier had no more than three surviving fighters.

Air-power and air defence were ever in his mind, and he knew that they must enjoy a higher priority in the Navy's planning or the Mediterranean Fleet – and the Home Fleet too perhaps – would be wiped out. Cunningham agreed whole-heartedly and drafted a long memorandum of complaint for Mountbatten to take back to London. He flew to Cairo a few days later in a Blackburn Skua of the Fleet Air

Arm, a machine that was obsolete even before it went into service, and was symptomatic of the state of that branch of the Navy. 'I'm afraid it was not terribly reliable,' the pilot recorded later, and remembered how anxious he was when Mountbatten refused a parachute.

The British Ambassador invited Mountbatten to dinner at the Embassy and was treated to a diatribe about the neglect of the RAF in the Middle East. Mountbatten took two weeks to fly to London, nearly twice as long as by sea in peacetime, so he had plenty of time to prepare in his mind the form of his offensive mission, beginning with Churchill. He did not get any firm promises, but it seemed highly appropriate that he should be offered the command of an aircraft carrier, which might give him the means of getting his revenge on the Luftwaffe. The *Illustrious*, whose berth the *Kelly* had occupied at Malta after the carrier was so badly bombed that she had to be sent to America, was completing her repairs at the US Navy Yard at Norfolk, Virginia. Until she was ready Churchill asked him to visit President Roosevelt and the US Navy bigwigs in Washington, to call on other influential people and to deliver lectures about the real nature of the war at sea. It was a roaring success, and Admiral Stark, the Chief of Naval Operations, asked him to visit Pearl Harbor and inspect its defences.

Mountbatten became a very considerable broadside in Churchill's more or less continuous barrage to get America into the war. The US Navy loved him, and only one feature of his tour dismayed them. He was horrified at the ease with which the massive base of Pearl Harbor could be attacked by surprise with, perhaps, the entire Pacific Battle Fleet concentrated and lined up neatly to be sent to the bottom. When Mountbatten gave Stark his forthright views on this, Stark commented with a laugh, 'I'm afraid putting some of your recommendations into effect is going to make your visit out there an expensive one for the Navy.' Ninety days later, with nothing done, the Japanese attacked.

Mountbatten heard the news not from the bridge of the *Illustrious* but from an office in Richmond Terrace, London. His sea-going fighting career had after all ended with the sinking of the *Kelly*. His destroyer days were over, his appointment to the *Illustrious*, with all its promise of excitement and of 'doing a "Beatty"', as he called it (i.e. matching that great Admiral's fame), cancelled.

Churchill had instead appointed him to Combined Operations, the first and very considerable step up the ladder to membership of the Chiefs of Staff Committee and two years hence to the Supreme Allied Command in South-East Asia.

'Begin with a small ship, a destroyer,' his father had advised him. 'It's the best way to start, and it will take you to the top in the end.' But he was still only forty-one when he was promoted acting Vice-Admiral *and* Lieutenant-General *and* Air Marshal.

'What a heavy burden is a name that becomes famous too soon,' claimed Voltaire; but Mountbatten found it featherlight for the remainder of his life.

Postscript

The loss of Greece and Crete, and so many ships and lives, together with German successes in North Africa, caused deep gloom and despondency in Britain in 1941. It was not until later that the German victories could be recognised as largely pyrrhic. In the battle for Crete, one of the most ferocious and hard-fought of the war for British and Imperial troops, the losses were about thirteen thousand killed, wounded and taken prisoner, with a further two thousand naval casualties, along with three cruisers, six destroyers sunk and severe damage to two battleships, a carrier and other smaller units.

The Allies also lost a valuable base in Crete, which could, theoretically, now become the launching base for further German incursions into Syria and south and west into Iraq and Persia (Iran) and the oil-rich Gulf.

This did not take place because Crete had become the locked door beyond which Germany could not penetrate. The reason for this was that the German 7th Airborne Division was broken, never to reform. Thanks to the heroic defence put up by the New Zealand, British and Australian forces, 'the Division was destroyed in Crete,' wrote Churchill. 'Upwards of five thousand of its bravest men were killed, thousands more wounded, and the whole structure of this organisation was irretrievably broken. It never appeared again in any effective form.' A further five to six thousand ground troops were lost at sea, victims of the Royal Navy which prevented the reinforcement of the Air Division by one soldier until the land battle was already lost. Moreover, the Navy also succeeded in bringing safely home from Crete in a second evacuation nearly seventeen thousand men to reinforce the hard-pressed desert army.

Evacuations, be they from Dunkirk, Norway, Crete or Greece, do not win wars, but the loss of territory, men and equipment has to be offset by other considerations.

Dunkirk lifted the spirit and determination of the nation as if the troops had returned from another Waterloo. The loss of Greece, and then Crete, was compensated for in two quite different ways. First, Britain and her allies impressed the neutral world by meeting her moral commitment in support of Greece while risking the loss of Egypt in doing so. It showed again Britain's will to fight on, which in turn influenced favourably the American Congress in its critical debate at this time on Lend-Lease, a measure that was essential if Britain was to go on fighting.

The stubborn defence in Greece and Crete, which held up great numbers of German troops as well as the now decimated 7th Airborne Division, led to the postponement of 'Barbarossa', the invasion of the Soviet Union, from the planned date of 15 May until 22 June. Those extra five and a half weeks of campaigning in fine weather could well have taken the German armies into Moscow and Leningrad, vital cities which were saved by the onset of winter.

That delay 'may well have made all the difference between German success and German failure in Russia', Lieutenant-Commander Peter Kemp, one-time Head of the Historical Section of the Admiralty, has written in his *Victory at Sea 1939–1945*.

The *Kelly*'s dead, and all those others who died at sea and on land, had been lost in the greatest cause of this century, the defeat of Hitler and his cruel tyranny.

Chronology of HMS Kelly

2 April 1937	Contract for construction signed with Messrs Hawthorn, Leslie, Hebburn-on-Tyne
26 August 1937	Keel laid
25 October 1938	Launched
23 August 1939	Commissioned
3 September 1939	War with Germany declared
4 September 1939	U-boat claimed probably sunk; not confirmed
12 September 1939	The Duke and Duchess of Windsor passengers from Cherbourg
17 September 1939	Rescues survivors from HMS *Courageous*
14 October 1939	U-boat claimed sunk; not confirmed
22 October 1939	Fails to intercept SS *City of Flint*
24 October 1939	Repairs from storm damage commence at Hebburn
14 December 1939	Repairs completed and leaves Hebburn
14 December 1939	Mined
15 December 1939	Repairs commence at Hebburn
28 February 1940	Repairs completed
2 March 1940	Collides with HMS *Gurkha*
13 March 1940	Repairs commence in London dockyard
27 April 1940	Repairs completed
29 April 1940	Evacuation of French troops from Namsos, Norway
9 May 1940	Torpedoed by E-boat
12 May 1940	Repairs commence at Hebburn
1 December 1940	Repairs completed
3 December 1940	Collides with SS *Scorpion*
15 January 1941	Damaged in storm; repairs commence at Devonport
24 April 1941	Arrives at Malta
14 May 1941	Bombards Benghazi
22 May 1941	Bombards Maleme airfield, Crete
23 May 1941	Sunk by Ju 87 dive-bombers approx. three miles off south-west coast of Crete

Appendix

The following list of losses of 'J' and 'K' class destroyers in which Mountbatten's 5th Flotilla is included indicates the vulnerability of this class of vessel in wartime:

Jersey	Mined Malta, 2 May 1941
Juno	Bombed Battle of Crete, 21 May 1941
Jupiter	Battle of Java Sea, 27 February 1942
Jaguar	U-boat, Mediterranean, 26 March 1942
Jackal	Dive-bombed, Mediterranean, 12 May 1942
Janus	Aircraft's torpedo, Anzio, 23 January 1944

Kelly } *Kashmir* }	Dive-bombed off Crete, 23 May 1941
Khartoum	Internal explosion, 23 June 1941
Kingston	Bombed Malta, 11 April 1942
Kandahar	Mined off Tripoli, 19 December 1942
Kipling	Bombed eastern Mediterranean, 11 May 1942

(*Javelin*, *Jervis*, *Kelvin* and *Kimberley* survived the war)

Bibliography

REAR-ADMIRAL D. ARNOLD-FORSTER, *The Ways of the Navy* (1931)

REAR-ADMIRAL W. S. CHALMERS, *The Life and Letters of David Beatty* (1951)

W. S. CHURCHILL, *The Second World War*, vol. 1 (1948)

JULIAN CORBETT, *Great War Naval Operations*, vol. 3 (1921)

ADMIRAL OF THE FLEET VISCOUNT CUNNINGHAM, *A Sailor's Odyssey* (1951)

CAPTAIN E. R. G. R. EVANS, *Keeping the Seas* (1919)

RICHARD HOUGH, *Louis and Victoria: The First Mountbattens* (1974)

RICHARD HOUGH, *Mountbatten: Hero of our Time* (1980)

LIEUTENANT-COMMANDER PETER KEMP, *Victory at Sea* (1957)

EDGAR J. MARCH, *British Destroyers* (1966)

W. PATTINSON, *Mountbatten and the Men of the Kelly* (1986)

KENNETH POOLMAN, *The Kelly* (1954)

REAR-ADMIRAL ANTHONY PUGSLEY, *Destroyer Man* (1957)

DENIS RICHARDS, *The Fight at Odds* (1953)

CAPTAIN S. W. ROSKILL, *The War at Sea*, vol. 1 (1954)

REAR-ADMIRAL G. W. G. SIMPSON, *Periscope View* (1972)

PHILIP ZIEGLER, *Mountbatten* (1985)

Index